Windows For Life

Inspirational And Devotional Illustrations

Don R. Yocom

CSS Publishing Company, Inc., Lima, Ohio

WINDOWS FOR LIFE

Copyright © 2004 by
CSS Publishing Company, Inc.
Lima, Ohio

All rights reserved. No part of this publication may be reproduced in any manner whatsoever without the prior permission of the publisher, except in the case of brief quotations embodied in critical articles and reviews. Inquiries should be addressed to: Permissions, CSS Publishing Company, Inc., P.O. Box 4503, Lima, Ohio 45802-4503.

Scripture quotations marked (NRSV) are from the *New Revised Standard Version of the Bible*, copyright 1989 by the Division of Christian Education of the National Council of the Churches of Christ in the USA. Used by permission.

Scripture quotations marked (NIV) are from the *Holy Bible, New International Version*. Copyright © 1973, 1978, 1984 International Bible Society. Used by permission of Zondervan Bible Publishers. All rights reserved.

Scripture quotations marked (KJV) are from the *King James Version of the Bible*, in the public domain.

Library of Congress Cataloging-in-Publication Data

Yocom, Don R., 1917-
　Windows for life : inspirational and devotional illustrations / Don R. Yocom.
　　p. cm.
Includes bibliographical references and index.
　ISBN 0-7880-2312-8 (pbk. : alk. paper)
　1. Homiletical illustrations. I. Title.
BV4225.3.Y63 2004
251'.08—dc22

2003026918

For more information about CSS Publishing Company resources, visit our website at www.csspub.com or e-mail us at custserv@csspub.com or call (800) 241-4056.

ISBN 0-7880-2312-8　　　　　　　　　　　　　　　　　　PRINTED IN U.S.A.

*This book is dedicated to my son,
David R. Yocom,
who has spent many hours on the
preparation of the manuscript,
thus making the book more readable.
Thanks, Dave.*

Table Of Contents

Topical Index   7

Introduction   17

Section I   19
   Humorous Windows For Life

Section II   45
   Great Windows For Life

Section III   117
   Hope Windows For Life

Section IV   119
   Conventional Wisdom Windows For Life
      Humorous One-liners
      Great Windows One-liners
      One-liners From Notable People

Topical Index

Topic	Number
Accountable	
Accountability	13
More Accountability	143
Adversity	
Colorful Pottery And Adversity	105
Thanks For The Boll Weevil	170
Advice	
Four Things A Man Must Do	116
Age	
Old Age — By Browning	147
Old Age — By Longfellow	148
America	
America Is Great, If	90
God Bless America	118
Arithmetic	
How Many Children	34
Playing The Numbers	54
Attendance	
Church Attendance	103
Church Attendance 2	104
Awareness	
Stab Us Awake	167
Better Living	
A Lesson In Mediocrity	84
Bible	
Is The Bible A Bank?	134
Selah	165
That Sunday School Class Teacher	171
The First Sunday School	175
The Holy Bible And Pitcairn Island	179
The Inspired Holy Bible	180

The Story Of Ben Hur	191
What Happened To Noah's Ark?	70
Brotherhood	
A Statue Honoring Prison Convicts	87
Brotherhood	100
The Good Neighbor	178
True Brotherhood	197
True Brotherhood 2	198
Character	
Being Like A Persimmon	98
Bringing Out The Best	99
Contrasts In Character	107
How Did You Play The Game?	130
Children	
Abstract Or Concrete	12
A Children's Prayer For A Bicycle	2
How A Child Thinks	128
Is God Left-handed?	39
On Saying Thanks	150
Who Made God?	212
Who is In Heaven	73
Christian	
A Christian Is	79
A True Christian	88
Four Things A Man Must Do	116
Christian Life	
W.W.J.D.	216
Christ's Love	
The Love Of Christ	182
Christmas	
Christmas Eve From Outer Space	102
Christmas For A College Girl	18
Whose Birthday?	74
Wise Men's Red Hats	75
The Church	
Church Attendance	103
Church Attendance 2	104

Most Unusual	144
Practical Christianity	156

Commitment
For A Dead Rabbit	113
He Gave His Lunch	125
Was It Luck Or "Pluck"?	202
What's Missing?	206

Cooperation
Teamwork	169

Courage
What One Man Can Do	205

Conscience
Conscience	106

Counselling
Strangers?	168

Cremation
Cremation, And An Old Saying	20

Criticism
How To Handle Criticism	131
The Fool Who Signed His Name	178

Dedication
Bringing Out The Best	99
For A Dead Rabbit?	113

Dishonesty
They Cooked The Books	194

Driving
Mother's Driving	45
Road Rage: He Drives Like Jehu	124
Those New Cars	68

Drunk
The Dog Knew Best	174

Easter
Ring Those Bells!	159

Ecumenical
An Ecumenical Leg	92

Education
Education And The Ends	109
The First Sunday School	175

Egotistical
   Like Swell Heads   43
Electronics
   Wahlstrom's Wonder   201
Embarrassment
   That Bag Of Cookies   57
   That Special Day   58
Eternity
   See Life
Evangelism
   Give Them Christ   117
Faith
   His Very Simple Credo   127
   The Print Of The Nails   189
   What If The Christian Faith Was Gone?   204
   Where Is God?   208
Faithful
   A Good Horse: The General   82
Father's Day
   Father's Day And The Trinity   111
Flowers
   Forgiveness   115
   Say It With Flowers   116
Friendship
   True Friendship   191
Funerals
   Funeral Customs   26
   Humor At A Funeral   37
Goals
   Beginning Again   96
   For A Dead Rabbit?   113
   What A Dream!   203
   Where Is Your Goal?   209
God
   A Pertinent Observation   86
   God Bless America   118
   God Knows!   119
   Is God Left-handed?   39

    Of What Kingdom Are You?   146
    Where Is God?   208
    Who Is The Architect?   211
    Who Made God?   212

Grace
    It's A Serendipity   136
    Music, A God-given Grace   145

Gratitude
    Gratitude At Sing Sing Prison   121
    Stab Us Awake!   167

Graciousness
    Being Gracious   97

Greatness
    America Is Great, If   90

Growth
    Growth   123
    Like A Candle   142

Health
    The Mayo Clinic   183

Heaven
    The Eastern Gate   218

Honesty
    A $10,000 Reward   76

Hope
    Finally, There Is Hope   217

Inspiration
    The Inspired Holy Bible   180

Investment
    An Investment In Eternity   95
    He Gave His Lunch   125
    Seed Investments   164
    The Seed Store   190
    When Henry Ford Gave A Dime   207

Jesus
    The Love Of Christ   182
    The Print Of The Nails   189
    W.W.J.D.   216

Joy
    Highways Of Happiness   126
Justice
    They Cooked The Books   194
Kindness
    An Act Of Kindness   91
    Kindness, by Dale Carnegie   139
    Kindness, by Emily Dickinson   140
Kingdom
    Of What Kingdom Are You?   146
Laughter
    A Drink Of Water   3
    A God-given Grace — Laughter   81
Lent
    Giving Up, In Lent   27
Life
    Eternity, From Thanatopis   110
    For A Dead Rabbit?   113
    How Do You Play The Game?   130
    Into Eternity   133
    The Four Levels Of Life   177
    Three Philosophies Of Life   196
Love
    An Expression Of Love   94
    Let's Roll! (No Greater Love Than This ...)   141
    Most Madly In Love   44
    Say, Who Do You Love?   162
    The Love Of Christ   182
Marriage
    That Wedding Ring   172
    Those Two Cents   195
Maturity
    Being Like A Persimmon   98
    Most Unusual   144
Mediocrity
    A Lesson In Mediocrity   84

Mercy
  A Kiss Of Mercy   83
Miracle
  Jesus' First Miracle   137
  The Miracle of Ice   184
  The Miracle Worker   185
Money
  A $10,000 Reward   78
  One American Dollar   151
Music
  God Bless America   118
  Music, A God-given Grace   145
  Music Off Key   46
  The Eastern Gate   218
Name
  How The Hot Dog Got Its Name   35
Needs
  Needs And Wants   48
New Year's
  On A New Year's Day   149
  Beginning Again   96
Noah's Ark
  A Bright Question   1
Observation
  A Pertinent Observation   86
One-liners
  Great Windows   B1-B194
  Humor   A1-A77
  From Notable People   C1-C60
Others
  See Brotherhood, also Kindness
  Puppies Can Share, Too!   157
  Three Philosophies Of Life   196
Pastors
  He Really Squeezed Them   29
  Pastor On Skates   52
  Super Religious   56

Patriotism
   Is This True Americanism?   135
Peace
   An Endless Line Of Splendor   93
   The International Garden Of Peace   181
   The Prince Of Peace   187
   The Prince Of Peace 2   188
Politics
   Election Time   22
   The Politicians' Prayer   63
Poverty
   Poor/Rich Boy   155
Power
   Keokuk's Answer   138
Prayer
   Channel One   101
   A Child's Prayer For A Bicycle   2
   God Uses Written Prayers, Also   120
   The Politicians' Prayer   63
Presence
   In The Presence Of God   132
   God Knows!   119
   With God At Antarctica   215
Publicity
   Church Attendance   103
   Church Attendance 2   104
Racism
   Cry, The Beloved Country   108
   Is This True Americanism?   135
Reality
   The Vale Of Paradise   192
Redemption
   Redemption And A Drop Of Water   158
   The Cleansing Fire   173
   Romans 8:28   160
   W(h)ite Out   210

Religion
    A Connectional Religion   80
Remembrance
    Ground Zero — One Year Later   122
Sacrifice
    Giving Up, In Lent   27
    He Gave His Lunch   125
Salvation
    The Cleansing Fire   173
    There's A Man On The Cross   192
Sanctification
    Second Springs   163
Service, To God
    A True Christian   88
Service To Man
    A Good Horse — The General   82
    How Did You Play The Game?   130
    The Mayo Clinic   183
    The People Had A Mind To Work   186
    What's Missing?   206
Soul
    A Living Soul   85
Stewardship
    He Gave His Lunch   125
    Pocketbook Protection   154
    Say It With Flowers   161
Taxes
    Who Really Pays The Tax?   213
Temptation
    Yield Not To Temptation   77
Terrorism
    Ground Zero — One Year Later   122
    Let's Roll   141
    Romans 8:28   160
Testimony
    The Story Of Ben Hur   191

Thanksgiving
  On Saying Thanks   150
Thoughtful
  Food For Thought   112
  Twentieth-Century Evaluation (T. S. Elliot)   200
  Selah   165
Time
  God's Time   28
  Some Good Things Take Time   166
Tradition
  How Did The Apostles Of Jesus Die?   129
Trinity
  Father's Day And The Trinity   111
Trust
  Our Total Trust In God   152
Unity
  An Ecumenical Leg   92
Way
  The Way (To The Post Office)   66
Wisdom
  Wisdom (President Coolidge)   214
Witness
  Give Them Christ!   117
  The Parable Of The Ten-inch Skillet   153
Work
  About Fishing   89
  Was It Luck Or "Pluck"?   202
Worthiness
  Parable Of The Ten-inch Skillet   153
Worship
  For Thoughtful Worship   114
  Like A Candle   142
Youth
  Not Couch Potatoes   50

Introduction

This book can be used for general reading as well as for providing illustrations for a sermon or a speech. Some topics can be used as devotional resources, and many of them are inspirational. A topical index is included for your convenience.

Windows For Life will also help us lighten a subject with humor, as well as enlighten the reader about it. Since life is both simple and complex, we present these "windows" so you can appreciate life more. They have been used in sermons intended to help people unravel the tangles in which we find ourselves sometimes.

Maybe a "one-liner" is what we need. We have several categories of them, some with a twist of humor as well as some with pathos.

I have not exhausted the sources of "windows for life"; they are all about us. We find them in the daily newspaper, especially on the comics page. Some of them have grown out of my daily experiences.

As a speaker, seeing an eyeful or listening to an earful and including what you saw or heard in a sermon or a speech can make what you present more pleasant.

For example, "a word aptly spoken is like apples of gold in settings of silver." That's Proverbs 25:11 (NIV). The book of Proverbs has a lot of these ideas in its "one-liners."

In this book, there are three kinds of "one-liners" in Section IV: Conventional Wisdom Windows For Life. Some are humorous and some are words aptly spoken or written. And there are also "one-liners" by noted speakers and authors that are "windows for life."

This book is for you to use and enjoy.

Don R. Yocom

Section I
Humorous Windows For Life

1. A Bright Question

What kind of lights were used on Noah's Ark?
Answer: How about "flood lights" or "arc lights"?

2. A Child's Prayer For A Bicycle

The little boy was praying quite loudly: "Oh, God, I would like to have a new bicycle!"

It was so loud that his father asked, "Why are you praying so loud? Is God deaf?"

The boy answered, "No, but Grandma is in the next room. And *she* is hard of hearing!"

3. A Drink Of Water

Dr. E. Stanley Jones, missionary evangelist in both India and the U.S., told us of the things he had seen behind the pulpit in churches where he had spoken. At one church beside a glass of water was this sign: "A drink of water might keep the sermon from being too dry."

And behind one pulpit there was a fire extinguisher. Dr. Jones commented: "What a tragedy! We have been putting out fires when we ought to be fanning the flames of the Spirit."

4. A Forrest Gump Story

Saint Peter saw Forrest Gump, a familiar name in the movies, at the entrance to Heaven. So the Gatekeeper to the blessed place decided to put Forrest on the spot. He told him he would have to answer three questions to get in.

Forrest nodded his approval.

Saint Peter asked, "First question: What two days of the week begin with the letter *T*?"

Gump answered, "Today and Tomorrow."

Saint Peter made the second question harder. He asked: "How many seconds are there in a year?"

Forrest quickly said, "Twelve."

Saint Peter inquired, "Why did you say twelve?"

Forrest answered, "January second, February second, March second, April second — on down to December second. That's twelve."

Then Saint Peter asked his third question: "What is God's first name?"

Forrest Gump answered, "Why, it's Andy!"

When Saint Peter heard the rest of Forrest's reply, he let him enter Heaven. It was, "We sing about it in Sunday school. 'Andy walks with me, Andy talks with me, Andy tells me I am his own!'"

5. A Kentucky Story (in fun, of course)

A visitor in a sixth grade classroom listened to the children answer questions from their teacher. She asked, "Who can recite the alphabet?"

She called on Billy, who started, "A, B, C, D, E, F, H, - J, - M --."

The teacher stopped him and asked, "Billy, why didn't you recite the whole alphabet?"

Billy answered, "I am from Kentucky."

The teacher then asked another student, Marianne, to recite the numbers from 1 to 25.

Marianne started, "1, 2, 3, 4, 5, 6, 7, 8, 9, 10, 11, 12, 13 -- 15 ---."

The teacher asked the eleven-year-old why she couldn't recite all the numbers from 1 to 25 without a mistake.

Marianne said, "I'm from Kentucky."

Then the teacher asked Charlie to recite the alphabet.

He said, "A, B, C, D, E, F, G, H, I, J, K, L, M, N, O, P, Q, R, S, T, U, V, W, X, Y, Z."

Everyone was pleased.

"Charlie," the teacher asked, "Count from 1 to 25."

He did: "1, 2, 3, 4, 5, 6, 7, 8, 9, 10, 11, 12, 13, 14, 15, 16, 17, 18, 19, 20, 21, 22, 23, 24, 25."

Everybody clapped their hands for Charlie, a sixth-grader, too.

Now the visitor asked Charlie, who had done better than Billy or Marianne, "Charlie, where you from?"

Charlie said, "I'm from Ohio."

Then the visitor asked, "How old are you?"

Charlie said, "I am sixteen years old."

6. A Mystery Story

A man worked in a factory where they made all kinds of garden tools; all the way from hand tools to ladders and wheelbarrows.

At the end of his shift one night, the man left the plant with a wheelbarrow load of sawdust. The watchman at the gate sifted through the sawdust with his hands, found nothing, and let him go through.

This happened several nights, but finally, he was arrested for stealing even when there was nothing in the sawdust. Why?

Answer: He was stealing the wheelbarrows.

7. A New Sunday School Building

At the ground-breaking ceremony for a new Sunday school building, children were also given the opportunity to turn over a shovelful of dirt. When one little girl got home and was asked what happened, she said: "Well, we dug for a new Sunday school, but we didn't find it!"

8. A Pastor's Humor

A young pastor with a sense of humor became a father; so at the county ministerial meeting he passed out "candy cigars." The baby was a boy.

A year later, we wondered what he would do when his wife gave birth to a baby girl.

But he was clever; at the next county ministerial association meeting, he passed out "Tootsie Rolls"!

9. A Real Pain

A pastor asked a friend if he would be willing to substitute in the pulpit of his church on a certain Sunday morning. The friend agreed to do so.

The friend came to the church and told the congregation he was like a piece of cardboard someone might stuff in a window if the glass had been broken. He would serve as a substitute.

After the service, as a woman was shaking hands with him, she said, "You were no substitute; you were a real pane (pain)!"

10. A Town Called Knockemstiff

Yes, it's a little town in the southwestern part of Ross County, Ohio. This is how the town got its name:

The pastor's little boy didn't like it when people went to sleep in the morning worship services. So one Sunday the boy brought his bean shooter and some beans with him to church. When asked, he told people, "If anyone goes to sleep in my dad's services, I'll Knockemstiff!"

The word got around, and not only was the church called Knockemstiff, but that's how the town got its name.

The Ohio Department of Transportation has had the name and location on their maps.

11. A True Substitute

There was once a trombone player who became too ill to march in a parade. The band director prevailed on a friend to march in the sick man's place and to fake playing the trombone.

Someone knew that friend, saw him in the parade, and later said to him: "Bill, I didn't know that you could toot on a trombone."

Bill answered him, "I was a substitoot!"

12. Abstract Or Concrete

A man had said he adored children and would do whatever he could for them. Then one day he had the concrete haulers come and pour a new concrete sidewalk in front of his house. Children nearby were curious and got into the freshly-poured concrete.

When the man found out about it, he was furious. A friend reminded him of what he had said about children. He answered: "I meant children in the abstract, not in the concrete!"

13. Accountability

"What kind of a place would this place be,
If everyone in it were just like me?"

This jingle reminds me of a story. A man named Sam had been fired at a business establishment. So Joe went to apply for a job.

Joe said to the man in the office, "I would like to apply for the vacancy Sam left."

The man at the desk answered, "Sam didn't leave a vacancy!"

14. Afraid In A Thunderstorm

There was a mother who, thinking her little girl would be frightened during a thunderstorm, went into the girl's room and got in bed with her, thinking sleeping there would make the child feel safe.

In the morning the little girl said: "All right, Mother; whenever you're frightened again, you can come and get into my bed with me!"

15. An Irish Story

Pat and Brigette dated a long time ...

Finally, Brigette asked Pat: "Don't you think we ought to get married?"

Pat answered, "Who'd want us?"

16. Another Mystery Story

A night watchman heard that his boss was going away on a long trip. He went to the office and warned his boss not to go on that trip, because the man had dreamed the previous night that the boss was in a bad accident.

The boss went on the trip, and there was no bad accident. When he returned to his business place, he fired the night watchman. Why?

Answer: A night watchman ought not sleep and dream.

17. Bad Chemistry

Here's to the memory of Willie.
Willie is no more:
What he thought was H_2O
Was H_2SO_4.

18. Christmas For A College Girl

Colleen, the college girl, had come home for the Christmas holiday. Next morning her mother was seated on the living room sofa when Colleen came from her bedroom, sat down, and snuggled up to her.

Mother said: "Colleen, when you were a little girl, you'd come to breakfast just the same way. You'd snuggle up to me and say, 'Cheerios, Mom, Cheerios.' "

The college girl murmured, "Master Card, Mom, Master Card!"

19. Cooties

The college professor in an astronomy class liked to use objects we all know to illustrate his lesson.

One class period he was teaching about our Universe, and particularly about our Sun, the Earth, and Mars.

He said: "To illustrate our lesson today, we will say that the globe on my desk is the Sun, that apple on Jack's desk is the earth, and my hat over on the hall tree is Mars. Any questions?"

A student inquired, "Is Mars inhabited?"

20. Cremation, And An Old Saying

Bill and Jake, from the rural countryside, went into the big city for their very first time. They saw a lot of buildings that were new to them. They finally came upon a place with a sign that read, Rose Hill Crematory. Neither of them knew what it meant.

Jake said, "I'll go inside and find out."

After a few minutes, the door opened and someone practically threw Jake out.

Bill asked, "What happened?"

Jake answered, "When I got inside, there were people standing around and not much going on. No one was talking. So I asked, 'What's cookin?' and they threw me out!"

21. Do You Need It?

Sign in a Vermont country store:
"If we haven't got it, you don't need it!"

22. Election Time

It was near election time when a pastor in Phoenix, Arizona, phoned the city's largest newspaper.

"Thank you," said he, "for the error you made in announcing on the church page my sermon topic for the past Sunday.

"The topic I sent in was, 'What Jesus saw in a Publican.' The paper reported, 'What Jesus saw in a Republican.'

"We had the biggest congregation this year!"

23. Entrance

Bill Collins had a small, but thriving, general store in a city. On both sides of his neat little store there were large businesses that seemed to dwarf the Collins' place.

They were famous well-known national stores with imposing brand names, but Bill Collins kept on serving the community.

"How do you do it?" he was asked. "Those other stores are so big!"

His answer was, "Look outside at the sign over the front door."
The sign had just one word: Entrance.

24. Eve And The Snake

In the story of Adam and Eve, Eve ate the wrong thing; she should have eaten the snake!
— From the book, *Puddin' Head Wilson* by Mark Twain

25. Freddie, The Flying Frog

Freddie, the frog, had a bright idea. After watching the geese flying south, he talked the geese into holding a stick between their legs, and he would bite into the middle of the stick, thereby getting a ride to warmer weather down south.

The trip began quite well. They took off slowly, and just as they began to rise, Freddie saw another frog down below him. He was so proud of his idea for travel, he opened his mouth to call to the one below, "See me fly ..." And you know what happened to the bragging frog.

The moral of the story: If you want to rise in life, keep your mouth shut about how smart you are!

26. Funeral Customs

An American and his Chinese friend were visiting a cemetery together. The American began poking fun at his friend by commenting, "When will your Chinese friend come up out of the ground and eat the food your people have left on top of the grave?"

The Chinese person answered, "When your American friend comes up out of the ground and smells the flowers your people have left on top of his grave!"

27. Giving Up, In Lent

During Lent, a certain man and his wife decided to give up drinking. They told their little son about it.

Later, they asked the son about what he had given up.

He said, "How about that beer you have been drinking?"

Father answered, "We meant giving up liquor, like brandy and whiskey — hard drinking!"

The son said, "Then I will give up hard candy!"

28. God's Time

Little Jimmy had lain on a hillock in the middle of a meadow one warm spring day. Watching the clouds, he began to think about God.

"God, are you really there?" Jimmy spoke out loud, and to his surprise a voice seemed to come down from the clouds.

"Yes, Jimmy, I'm here. What can I do for you?"

Answering back quickly, Jimmy said, "God, what is a million years like to you?"

God responded in terms Jimmy might understand. "A million years to me, Jimmy, is like a minute."

"Okay," said Jimmy. "Well, then, what's a million dollars like to you?"

"A million dollars is like a penny to me," God answered.

"Wow!" remarked Jimmy, who then had a bright idea. "You're so generous ... can I have one of your pennies?"

God replied, "Sure thing, Jimmy! Wait a minute!"

29. He Really Squeezed Them

A side show at the traveling circus which came to town featured a guy who squeezed a lemon very hard and then offered to onlookers a $10 reward if they could squeeze it and get any more juice out of it.

Several people tried, but had no results.

Then a man came forward and asked if he could try to get more juice out of it. He was given the lemon and squeezed two more drops out of it. The side show operator asked, "How did you do that? No one else has ever squeezed more juice out of the lemon than I had squeezed before."

The man answered, "We have just finished raising a lot of money for our church building campaign. I'm the pastor!"

30. Hillbilly Humor

A man was sitting in front of a typical village in the southeastern Ohio hills, when some guys drove up and stopped.

One asked: "How long has this town been dead?"

The villager responded: "Well, not very long; you're the first buzzards we've seen!"

31. Hit It With The Hammer

Devere Allen used to tell this story.

There was a blacksmith who hired a boy to work with him in his shop. The boy was not very bright. In getting started, the smith was showing the boy what to do.

Said he: "First, I place the horseshoe on the anvil. Then when I nod my head, hit it with the hammer."

The boy hit the blacksmith hard on the head!

32. Holy Water

I asked a Roman Catholic priest in Delphos, Ohio, how they make "Holy Water."

He said, "Use tap water and boil the Hell out of it!"

33. Hot Dog, This Is It!

Someone asked an ex-alcoholic what the word "hallelujah" meant.

He replied: "I don't know, but I think it means 'Hot dog, this is it!' "

34. How Many Children?

At a hospital waiting room, three men waited while their wives were to give birth to children. It was in the state of Minnesota. One man was a ball player, and the other two were salesmen.

When the nurse announced to the ball player that his wife had given birth to twins, he commented: "It figures; I'm a ball player for the Minnesota Twins!"

Then another nurse came and told the second man that his wife had given birth to triplets. He said, "I work for the 3M Corporation, Minnesota Mining and Manufacturing; it figures!"

When the third nurse came to report to the third man, also a salesman, he was greatly agitated. Why?

He worked for 7-Up.

35. How The Hot Dog Got Its Name

A little dog followed its owner to his bakery, and got inside the place. The doggie's name was Fido.

There once was a dog named Fido,
He went to sleep on some pie dough.
The cook said, "Don't wake him,
I'll bake him! HOT DOG!"

36. Humility

A French monk bemoaned the fact that his monastic order was not as famous as the Jesuits for their scholarship or the Trappists for silence and good works.

"But," he added, "when it comes to humility, we're tops!"

37. Humor At A Funeral

At the funeral of famous Senator Barry Goldwater, broadcast live on the PBS public television, the brother of Barry told this true story:

The Goldwater family owned a department store in Phoenix, Arizona, and both of the brothers worked there.

Maybe you will remember when department stores had a central office. At each department sales desk there would be a cage containing conveyers in which the money of a sale would be placed with the bill. Then it was drawn through a vacuum tube to the central office. Once received there, a receipt would be returned by a reverse process to the sales desk.

One day, the brother observed Barry walking cautiously through an aisle. Suddenly he stooped down, grabbed a mouse by the tail, took it to the nearest sales desk, put it in a conveyor, and sent it to the financial office! You can guess the remainder of the story.

The description by Barry's brother was hilarious, and those present for the funeral had a good laugh.

And I think Barry would have had fun, too, if he could have attended that funeral service.

38. Ignition Blinds

The fellow was a school dropout who worked as a mechanic in a garage. He didn't know much about things around the house.

One day he asked the garageman if he could have some time off to go shopping with his wife.

"What for?" asked the garageman.

The guy said, "My wife wants to buy some ignition blinds for our house."

39. Is God Left-handed?

"God is left-handed," the little child told her preacher.

He asked, "How do you know?"

She said, "The Bible says that Jesus sat on God's right hand!" (Mark 16:19 KJV).

"Also," the girl added, "in Acts 7:55 (KJV) we read, 'Jesus standing on the right hand of God.' "

40. Is Punctuation Important?

What did Shakespeare say?
"Woman, without her man, is nothing!"
"Woman, without her, man is nothing!"

41. It's Shortening

A man who was not tall and muscular asked a friend what he could do to make himself taller and more muscular. His friend answered, "Go home and rub some grease on your chest."

The man tried it for a week and nothing happened.

When he saw his friend again, he told him how he had tried rubbing some grease on his chest, but it didn't make him taller or more muscular.

His friend asked, "What grease did you use?"

The man said, "Crisco."

The friend said, "That won't work. Crisco is shortening."

42. Lightning Bugs

Some Boy Scouts were camping in a rather swampy area. It was bedtime and the boys went to their tents to get away from the swarm of mosquitoes.

Then the lightning bugs came. One of the scouts said: "I give up. They're even coming at us with flashlights!"

43. Like Swell-heads

Two purebred dogs were walking daintily down the street. They met a big alley dog. Embarrassed at meeting such company, to get away, one of them said, "We must go, but my name is Mimi: M-I-M-I." The other purebred dog said, "My name is Fifi: F-I-F-I."

The alley dog put up his nose and responded: "My name is Fido, spelled P-H-Y-D-E-A-U-X."

44. Most Madly In Love?

It was reported that a famous football star, class of 2002, had fallen in love with a beautiful girl, and began following her around one evening. Finally, the coed turned around and asked him, "Why do you keep following me?"

He declared, "Because you are the loveliest person I have ever met. I have fallen madly in love with you. I might even ask you to marry me!"

"Okay," she said, "but you have merely to look behind you to see my younger sister, who is ten times more beautiful than I am."

The guy turned around and saw a very homely gal instead of a beautiful girl.

He yelled, "You lied to me!"

She retorted, "So did you. If you were so much in love with me, why did you turn around?"

45. Mother's Driving

A school teacher was discussing highway safety and advised the children that once they started crossing a street they should never look back. She said, "In the Bible we read about Lot's wife: she looked back and turned into a pillar of salt."
A child spoke up, "Teacher, I was out in our car with my mother last week. She looked back and turned into a telephone pole."

46. Music, Off Key

One Sunday morning, at a neighborhood church, the choir was singing way off key. Someone commented: "It sounded like a 'moron' tabernacle choir."

47. My Precinct

When they were giving out flu shots one year, a poor lady had tried to get hers at the Red Cross building, but they told her they couldn't give her the treatment. So she went to the hospital emergency room. There she explained to the lady at the desk, "I came here because I didn't know what part of me is my precinct."
The emergency desk lady asked, "Would you say that again, please?"
The poor lady said, "When I went to the Red Cross, they told me I would have to get my flu shot in my precinct. What is my precinct?"

48. Needs And Wants

After I had preached a sermon on the difference between "needs and wants," on our way home from church, we passed an ice cream store. My five-year-old said, "Hey, Dad, I need an ice cream come!"

49. Noah's Ark

Remember: Noah's Ark was built by amateurs,
   The Titanic was built by professionals.

50. Not Couch Potatoes

Recently, people who watch television most of the time have been called "Couch Potatoes." Have you heard the expression?
Then what do you call children who watch television a lot?
Not Couch Potatoes. Try "Tatertots."

51. On Playing Hookey

A little boy was crying, and someone asked him what was the matter. He said, "I've been playing hookey from school all day, and I just found out today is Saturday!"

52. Pastor On Skates

A wealthy woman entered Heaven, and Saint Peter produced a bicycle for her to ride on the golden streets. But she soon observed her former maid on earth go by in a Cadillac, and the neighbor's former gardener was driving a Rolls Royce.
She looked at Saint Peter and asked why those people were doing so well in Heaven.
Saint Peter said, "The kind of transportation you get in Heaven depends on how good a Christian you were on earth."
She agreed both the maid and the gardener had worked hard on earth and deserved what they now had in Heaven.
Two days later the lady again met Saint Peter, and she was laughing.
"What's so funny?" he asked.
"Yesterday," she said, "I saw my former pastor going by on roller skates!"

53. Patience, Dear!

Husband shouting at wife: "For the last time, are you ready to go?"

"For Heaven's sake, be quiet," said the wife. "I've been telling you for the last hour that I'll be ready to go in a minute!"

54. Playing The Numbers

A woman entered a guessing game at a store to win a new refrigerator. She won the game by guessing the correct number, which was 51. When asked how she decided on 51, she replied: "I have always liked the number 7, and I guess since 7 x 7 is 51, I used that number to win!"

55. Six Pieces Or Eight Pieces?

A guy was ordering a pizza by telephone, when the man on the phone asked: "How shall we cut the pizza?"

The guy answered, "You'd better cut it in six pieces; I don't think I can eat eight pieces!"

56. Super Religious

The story is being told that Billy Graham, Oral Roberts, and Bob Schuller were to be received into heaven.

But due to a housing project not finished on time, they were sent to that "other place."

After a week, Satan was fit to be tied. Graham was converting demons to Christ, Roberts was healing the sick, and Schuller was in the process of air-conditioning the place!

57. That Bag Of Cookies

The other day a businessman reported to an airport, purchased his ticket, and was checked through carefully. He had some time to wait, so he bought a bag of cookies and a newspaper. Placing his briefcase beside him, he settled down in the waiting area and began reading his newspaper.

Another traveler came in and sat in the next seat beyond the light stand. After several minutes the first man heard the rustling sound of a paper bag and looked out of the corner of his eye to see the stranger with his hand in a bag of cookies on the light stand. The stranger took a cookie and began eating it.

Traveler 1 thought, "Wow! I must not create a scene, but those cookies ... After all!"

So he put his hand also in the cookie bag, took a cookie, and began eating it.

Then the other man took another cookie out of the bag. What about that! One by one the two men helped themselves down to the last cookie. The other guy broke it in half and offered our friend a piece of it. Then it was time for the second traveler's flight.

Soon, it was time for the first traveler to board his plane and he was on his way. Settled in his seat, he opened his briefcase and there was his bag of cookies! He had forgotten he had put them there! Wow!

58. That Special Day

As a man was leaving for his office on a wintry day, his wife hinted, "Tomorrow is a special day, you know!"

At his office he thought it over, wondering what special day she meant. "Why, tomorrow must be our anniversary! We were married on a wintry day!" he thought to himself.

So he immediately ordered a dozen red roses to be delivered the next day, and made reservations at the best restaurant in town.

That evening his wife said, "You know, Ted, tomorrow will be different. Instead of having beef steak or chicken for dinner, we will eat sausage. After all, it is a special day: it's Ground Hog Day!"

59. The Cuckoo Clock

A man stayed out so late one night that when he quietly came into the bedroom, the cuckoo clock struck two; so he went and made the cuckoo sound ten more times.

At breakfast his wife said, "Dear, the cuckoo clock needs fixing."

"Oh, is that so?" he answered.

"Yes," she said, "last night it cuckooed two times, then it hiccupped once, and then it cuckooed ten more times!"

60. The Doctor's Fee

A man carried his dog into the vet's office, and after an examination the doctor told him the dog was dead.

"Are you sure?" asked the man.

The vet had some pets in his place, so he brought a cat in and held it over the dog. Nothing happened.

Again the doctor said, "Your dog is dead."

The man was still not satisfied; so the vet had another pet, a Labrador retriever, come in the room. The Lab just sniffed and walked away.

The man said, "Okay, how much do I owe you?"

The doctor answered, "$650."

The man objected. "Fifty dollars should be enough for an office call!"

The vet then said, "Fifty dollars for the office call, $300 for the cat scan, and $300 for the lab test. $650 total."

61. The Hereafter

An elderly lady confided in her pastor that lately she was bothered by the "hereafter."

The pastor said, "Why, Mary, you should not have to worry about death and Heaven since you are a Christian."

She answered, "That's not what I mean: when I go to the basement for a can of food, I get there only to ask myself, 'What am I here after?' Or, I go upstairs to get a blanket, and when I get there I have to ask myself, 'What am I here after?' "

62. The Meaning Of Amen

During a children's sermon, Rev. Larry Eisenberg asked the children: "What is the meaning of 'Amen'?"
A little boy put up his hand and said, "It means, 'Tha - tha - tha -that's all, folks'!"

63. The Politicians' Prayer

Two politicians were arguing about something when the first one said: "I'll bet you $5 that you can't pray The Lord's Prayer."
The other politician answered by praying:

"Now I lay me down to sleep,
   I pray the Lord my soul to keep.
If I should die before I wake,
   I pray the Lord my soul to take. Amen."

The first politician handed over a $5 bill and said, "Here's $5. I didn't think you knew it!"

64. The Preacher's Parrot

A lady bought a parrot from a retired sailor. It had one bad habit: it used swear words sometimes. She wanted to break him of the habit.
There was a parsonage next door, and one day a different pastor moved in, and he owned a parrot. The lady got a bright idea and talked to the minister about it.

She said: "My parrot used to belong to a sailor, and the bird picked up the bad habit of using swear words. I would like to borrow your parrot and put its cage next to my parrot's cage. Maybe your parrot would help me break my parrot's bad habit of swearing."

It was agreed, so the cages were placed side by side in the lady's living room. There was a lot of chattering until she covered them for the night.

Next morning, the lady uncovered the cages, and her parrot swore at her as usual, and then said, "Good morning, I wish you were dead!"

The preacher's parrot, in a solemn, deep tone, slowly said, "Ah-h-h men!"

65. The Smart Old Indian Chief

Some curious tourists stopped along an Arizona road where they saw an old Indian chief sitting in front of his teepee. He was all decked out with Indian clothing and feathers. His teepee was also. There was a sign on the teepee:

Ask Any Question
I Will Answer
$5.00

So one of the tourists asked the old chief: "What did President Calvin Coolidge have for breakfast, June 29, 1920?"

The Indian chief answered, "Eggs."

They thought that was okay for a person in the White House, so they paid the chief $5.

Several years later, one of the travelers was on that same road and saw the old Indian chief with his teepee and sign. He decided to humor the old man, so he stopped his car and approached the chief. In typical Indian lingo, the tourist asked, "How?"

The Indian chief answered, "Scrambled!" Then he added, "Five dollars, sir!"

66. The Way

A little boy, while walking down the street, met a stranger who asked him, "Can you tell me the way to the Post Office?"

The little boy said, "Yes, go that way to the next street, turn to the right, and you will see it."

The stranger, who was an evangelist, thanked the boy, and then said, "Come over to the United Methodist Church tonight to the meetings, and I'll show you the way to Heaven."

The boy shook his head and answered, "No, I don't think so; you don't even know the way to the Post office!"

67. The Woman's Purse

A woman left her purse in a big city church, so the next day the pastor brought it to her at her own home. He had driven up in a new Cadillac automobile. As he gave to her the purse, it fell open and a pack of cigarettes dropped out.

The pastor said, "Jesus Christ would never have smoked cigarettes!"

The woman answered, "Yes, that's true. But Jesus never rode around in a brand new Cadillac, either!"

68. Those New Cars!

The Governor of Michigan was invited as a guest of honor to an automobile factory. While he was there they assembled a car in exactly 22 minutes. The matter was given considerable publicity in the news media.

A month or so later, an obviously angry man called on the telephone and wanted to talk with the CEO of the car company. When the officer asked why, the angry man said, "Is it true that, in honor of the governor, your factory put a car together in 22 minutes?"

"Absolutely true," the CEO replied.

The guy shouted on the phone, "I'm mad! I've got that car!"

— Reported in a Michigan newspaper

69. Try, Try Again

A child prayed: "O God, make me a good girl, and if at first you don't succeed, try, try, again."

70. What Happened To Noah's Ark?

There has been a lot of speculation for some time. Read on ...
When the flood subsided, his wife asked Noah, "What are you going to do with the Ark?"
He said, "I left the termites on board!"

71. What Moses Said

This story came from a tour guide in Israel:
It seems that when the Lord finished the Ten Commandments, he had trouble finding someone to take them.
You have seen those pictures of Moses with two tablets of stone on which are shown Roman Numerals I to X carved thereon.
When the Arabians were approached about taking the commandments, they turned down the opportunity, because they wanted to have as many wives as they liked, and the Seventh Commandment bothered them.
And the stone masons also refused the offer, because they often made idols out of stone. Other cultural groups had excuses.
When the Lord asked Moses if he would have them, he bargained, "How much are they?"
The Lord said, "They're free!"
Moses answered, "I'll take two!"

72. Who Am I?

At a nice old folks home it was reported that the President of the United States had entered to visit, saw a nice-looking old lady in the parlor near the reception desk, went over, and sat down beside her.

They talked about the weather and about her health and about some other generalities. Then he said to her, "Ma'am, do you know who I am?"

She took his hand, patted it, and said, sweetly, "I am sorry I don't, but if you go over there to the office desk, they can tell you who you are!"

73. Who Is In Heaven?

We lived for four years in Delphos, Ohio, which is a predominately Roman Catholic town. The joke these residents liked to tell the most on themselves, more than any other one, was this one:

A man died and went to Heaven. He was given a tour of the place by Saint Peter who said, "We will visit Church Street first."

As they walked, Saint Peter pointed out some of the church buildings.

"That's the United Methodist Church and here now is the Baptist Church; then on down the way, the Lutherans." They passed other churches and Saint Peter would call them by name.

"Now be quiet as we pass this building," he said.

After passing it, the visitor asked, "Why were we supposed to be quiet?"

Saint Peter answered, "They are the Roman Catholics, and they don't think there is anyone else in Heaven but them!"

74. Whose Birthday?

It was gift unwrapping time on Christmas morning, and Grandma asked her little granddaughter if she had received all she wanted for Christmas.

The child answered: "No, but it wasn't my birthday!"

75. Wise Men's Red Hats

A visitor to a certain town noticed many homes had Christmas nativity scenes in front of them. But there was something about them different from what you usually see. In all of the scenes the three Wise Men were wearing bright red firemen's hats!

The visitor asked a native about it: "Sir, I admire the nativity scenes in your town, but isn't it unusual that in all those displays the three Wise Men were wearing bright red hats?"

The native answered, "It's based on the Bible story where it said, the three Wise Men came from a-'far.'"

76. Without One Flea

Another little girl was singing at church, "Just as I am, without one flea."

77. Yield Not To Temptation

Mother: "Tommy, did you go swimming in the creek when I said, 'No'?"

Tommy: "Yes, Mom; the other boys went in, so I did, too."

Mother: "Did you have a bathing suit?"

Tommy: "Yeah, I wore it under my clothes, just in case!"

Section II
Great Windows For Life

78. A $10,000 Reward!

Some years ago in Los Angeles, California, a Brinks armored truck used to transport money dropped a bag that contained $240,000. An honest man, a janitor by the name of Douglas Johnson, found it and took it to the bank. Brinks gave him a $10,000 reward for what he did.

"But," said Mr. Johnson, "I wished I'd never seen the bag and returned it. I received letters and phone calls for being dumb and stupid. I've had to listen to it every day of the week since I gave the money back. It has made me a *poor* man!"

How would you deal with a thing like that?

79. A Christian Is

A mind through which Christ thinks,
A heart through which Christ loves,
A voice through which Christ speaks,
A hand through which Christ helps others.

80. A Connectional Religion

It is a well-known fact that a shoe store salesman won Dwight L. Moody to Christ. That started an interesting chain of events.

Moody literally touched the hearts of a great multitude of people with his down-to-earth language set on fire for the Lord.

While Moody was in England, an English medical student, working on his doctorate, was called by God's Spirit, in one of

Moody's meetings. Trained to be a medical missionary, he spent his life working with people of Labrador, he also was given the title of Sir Wilfred Grenfell. He then won John R. Mott to become a Christian.

Mott started, early in the twentieth century, the famous Student Volunteer Movement, that reached multitudes of college-age youth for Christian missions.

His leadership touched the lives of those who had a dream of a World Council of Churches. Years passed, and with the cooperation of many Christian leaders, the World Council had come into existence and continues today. And the chain goes on ...

Christianity is a connectional religion, and we who call ourselves Christians are bound together in it, regardless of denominational titles, and want to pass it on. No wonder it is one of the four great religions on Earth.

81. A Gift Of God's Grace — Laughter

Humankind is never so expressive of the goodness of God as when a person is laughing. In the Holy Bible, Ecclesiastes 3 states that "for everything there is a season and a time to every purpose under Heaven ... there is a time to laugh" (portions of verses 1 and 3).

One has only to listen to a small child bubbling over with joy to understand how natural it can be to laugh.

Surely part of our praise to Almighty God for his eternal goodness can be laughing as well as singing. The two seem to complement each other.

Proverbs says, "A merry heart is good like a medicine."

Humor can be used in various ways to clarify a spiritual problem. Though it is said that there is no biblical expression of laughter by Jesus Christ, Jesus did use irony, a form of humor. In the story of the woman who had been caught in adultery, she had been brought to Jesus for his condemnation. When Jesus said, "Anyone among you who is without sin, be the first to throw a stone at her" (John 8:7 NRSV), no one cast a stone! We smile at that.

We also know that Jesus enjoyed festive occasions, and at such times there is always harmless banter, person to person, with laughter following. If he did not laugh, Jesus must have enjoyed others who felt like laughing. People enjoy having a good time together.

Norman Cousins, former editor of *Saturday Review*, experienced a serious illness and discovered for himself what humor can do for one's spirit.

Later, he wrote about it and gave lectures about how laughter can help a person in times of recovery from illness and depression.

We think of all those people whose humorous speaking and writing have blessed us all. Mark Twain was our first American classical humorist. More recently, Will Rogers was a favorite in his time. It is said that Rogers made even President Calvin Coolidge, noted for his glumness, enjoy laughing at Will's jokes.

Many comedians we could name, like Red Skelton, Jack Benny, Fred Allen, and the famous redhead comedienne of television fame, Lucille Ball, all have made life more endurable.

A little girl was reported to have asked her mother, "Will Red Skelton go to Heaven when he dies?"

The mother answered, "I suppose so."

The child said, "Won't God laugh!"

In the give and take of general conversation, humor often comes naturally, as we account the events of the day, some of which could have been downright funny.

One of the most popular features of the daily newspaper is the comics page. There we meet *Dennis the Menace*, *Peanuts*, *Blondie and Dagwood*, and *The Family Circus*.

This world would be a sad place if we couldn't enjoy laughter and see the humorous side of life. We need more of it.

82. A Good Horse: The General

The tenth President of the United States was John Tyler. President Tyler had a horse he named The General. An epitaph was carved on the gravestone of that horse. It reads:

> "Here lies the body of my good horse.
>   The General
> For twenty years he bore me around the circuit of my practice, and in all that time he never made a blunder.
> Would that his master could say the same!"

83. A Kiss Of Mercy

The well-known outstanding Christian layman and U.S. Senator from Oregon, Harold Hughes, some years ago was seated at a prayer breakfast with 500 guests he was soon to address. Suddenly, accidentally, a waitress spilled a cake and lemon sauce dessert on him, and was forced to clean up the mess before all those people.

When she finally did finish the cleanup task, the good Senator surprised her by drawing her still-red face down to him and giving her a kiss of appreciation.

A smile returned to the face of the young waitress as she left the room, restored by a kiss of loving kindness by the very one she had so rudely disturbed.

A friend of ours, Dr. Myron Augsburg, then President of Eastern Mennonite College, who had witnessed the event, said he realized then that the young woman would tell her story of forgiveness by the Senator the rest of her life. What any of her apologies could have done for her, that act of mercy did it all.

Dr. Augsburg reminds us that the one who can redeem a situation is the one who has been hurt. Jesus did so by his act of forgiveness on the cross.

Can we accept the example the next time we are hurt, and set free the whole matter by being just as merciful as Senator Harold Hughes, or Jesus Christ?

84. A Lesson In Mediocrity

A man had a bushel of early apples, the kind that spoil easily. His friend smiled at him, because he would always take out the apples which had soft and rotten spots and use them first. As a result he used only half rotten apples until the bushel was gone.

Is that a lesson in living! How about the gossipers who spend their time talking about the faults of someone they knew, and never get around to commending the better examples of persons we might know. What an example of mediocrity!

Or is it an example of the news media that emphasize the sordid ways some people live, but those who live wholesome lives are never reported.

Which shall we choose? Half spoiled or unspoiled?

P.S. I used this "window of life" in a sermon and had a lady tell me she had always taken the half rotten apples first, thinking that was the way to use them. She had missed the point of what I was telling.

85. A Living Soul

"The social being without the personal being is a body without a soul;
The personal being without the social being is a soul without a body;
One is a corpse, and the other is a ghost;
Put them together and they make a living soul."
— E. Stanley Jones

86. A Pertinent Observation

The poet Elizabeth Barrett Browning wrote:

Earth crammed with Heaven,
And every common bush afire with God;
And only he who sees takes off his shoes,
The rest stand around the pick blueberries.

87. A Statue Honoring A Prison Convict

Yes, it is in Crestline, California, and it is a composite figure with eyes of an Oriental, nose of an African-American, mouth and chin of a white person. In its hand there is a fire axe.

In the 1950s a government honors camp for prison convicts was built at Pilot Rock near Crestline. There was local reaction against it being there.

But there came a day when forest fires threatened Crestline, and the convicts were allowed to fight the fire. Nisei Americans, blacks, and whites fought side by side, and finally won their fight.

Today, Crestline has this odd statue, the only one of its kind, dedicated to human brotherhood and in honor of prison convicts.

88. A True Christian

In the Armenian-Turkish War in Europe early in the twentieth century, an Armenian nurse discovered one day that a Turkish patient in the hospital where she worked was the man who had killed her father during a battle. She continued as a faithful nurse in her treatment of that man.

When her Turkish patient found out who she was and that he had killed her father, he asked her why she had not tried to kill him.

Her answer was, "I am a Christian."

89. About Fishing

Sitting still and fishing makes no person great;
the Good Lord sends the fish, but you must dig the bait.

90. America Is Great, If

Alexis de Tocqueville, the French historian, after an exhausting study, once said:

"I sought for the greatness and genius of America in her commodious harbors and the simple rivers and it was not there.
I sought for the greatness and genius of America in her fertile fields and boundless forests, and it was not there.
I sought for the greatness and genius in her rich mines and her world commerce, and it was not there.
I sought for the greatness and genius in her public school system and her institutions of learning, and it was not there.
I sought for her greatness and genius in her democratic Congress and her matchless Constitution, and it was not there.
Not until I went into the churches of America and heard from her pulpits aflame with righteousness did I understand the secret of her genius of power.
America is America because America is *good*, and if America ever ceases to be good, America will cease to be great!"

How prophetic!

91. An Act Of Kindness

When Bob Howard was the Sheriff of Darke County, Ohio, he and his wife had an interesting custom. Every Sunday morning, after attending church services, they would go to the county jail and bring out one of the teenagers who had been incarcerated the night before for some typical offenses: drunk driving, or creating a spectacle in some nightclub, and so forth.

They would have that teenager join them at their dinner table at noon for a good Sunday dinner. What a surprise! Nothing would be said about why the individuals had been brought to the jail. They would be treated like family. They could see that the sheriff was a kind and loving man, and his wife his supporter.

Bob told the Darke County Ministerial Association how often the youth would break down and tell how sorry they were for what they had done.

At least one high school girl I counselled considered it the kindest thing anyone had ever done for her. (Read Mark 1:41 in the Bible.)

92. An Ecumenical Leg

There's a wonderful story about a doctor who had among his patients an elderly Roman Catholic lady whose income was quite limited. For health reasons she had a leg amputated and needed an artificial leg.

Among the doctor's patients had been a United Methodist man who had passed away about that time, and left behind a so-called "wooden leg."

Yes, it turned out that the man's leg was the right length and would fit the needs of the lady.

So the doctor, with the approval of the man's family, fitted the leg to the woman. It all worked out beautifully, an example of human brotherhood. A Methodist leg replaced the Roman Catholic lady's sick body member, making it possible for her to go anywhere she wanted to go.

93. An Endless Line Of Splendor

Vachel Lindsay wrote:

An endless line of splendor
    These troops with Heaven for home,
This is our faith tremendous.
    Our wild hope, who shall scorn,
That in the name of Jesus
    The world shall be reborn!

94. An Expression Of Love

An American journalist during World War II watched a Roman Catholic sister, who was a nurse, cleanse the gangrenous sores of a wounded soldier.

The journalist exclaimed: "I wouldn't do that for a million dollars!"

The nurse, without stopping or looking up, said, "Neither would I!"

95. An Investment In Eternity

Herbert Hoover was a poor boy working his way through Stanford University in California. One year, as chairman of a lecture and concert committee, he engaged the famous concert pianist Paderewski for a concert for a sum of money. Due to bad weather they did not take in enough money to pay the guest musician, but he generously said, "Don't worry about it."

Years later, Mr. Paderewski was the premier of Poland, after World War I. Mr. Hoover was the American who was sent to Europe with food for hungry people. He walked into the Premier's office and told Mr. Paderewski he was there to repay his debt back from his college days. The check Herbert Hoover gave to Mr. Paderewski was worth $5 million dollars!

In accepting the gift, the great Premier said, "Is this not a good illustration of that old saying from our Holy Book that 'bread cast upon the waters shall return, thou shalt find it after many days' " (Ecclesiastes 11:1)?

Mr. Hoover later became the President of the U.S.A.; that food gift was an investment in eternity.

96. Beginning Again

The poet Louise Tarkington once wrote:

I wish there were some wonderful place
    Called the "Land of Beginning Again"
Where all our mistakes and all of our heartaches
    And all of our poor selfish grief
Could be dropped, like a shabby old coat at the door,
    And never put on again.

97. Being Gracious

One time, John Wesley, who started the Methodist Church, was calling in the home of a wealthy Englishman. While they were visiting, the man's daughter came into the room where they were in conversation. She was bedecked with bangles and jewels.

The man spoke harshly: "See my daughter's hand? It's covered with jewels!"

Mr. Wesley took the hand of the daughter and said, "It's a lovely hand!"

So surprised was the daughter that she went to hear Wesley preach, and gave her heart to Christ.

98. Being Like A Persimmon

In the autumn time, a persimmon tree, loaded with its golden purple fruit, is a sight to behold. One is tempted to eat one of the fruit, juicy and somewhat sweet, only to discover that at this time of the year it will pucker your mouth and leave a bitter taste.

Unlike other fruit, it takes harsh freezing weather to bring out the best taste it can give. In other words, persimmons can take it, when other fruit would be lost.

Through the years I have known some people who were like a fully-mature persimmon. They have experienced hard and tough times that hurt even to one's soul, but by the grace of God they made it clear through. These persimmon-like people become more and more delightful in their maturity.

Maybe we could pray and strive to become more like a fully-ripe persimmon.

99. Bringing Out The Best

A wealthy businessman had acquired a Cremona violin, reportedly one of the best violins ever made. He asked Fritz Kreisler to play it for him.

After Mr. Kreisler had given a fine rendition of an excellent musical selection, the businessman told Kreisler: "Please keep the violin. It belongs to you! You can bring out of it the best that can be done."

We belong to Christ. He alone can bring out of our lives the very best. That is our hope.

100. Brotherhood

I sought my soul, my soul I could not see.
I sought my God, my God eluded me.
I sought my brother, and I found all three.
— Anonymous

101. Channel One

Not being a television electronic designer, I do not know why all television sets begin with Channel 2. In recent years many more channels have been added, but none ever uses number 1.

What is Channel One? I call it *Prayer*.

Prayer is far superior to any other communications channels. It is universal and exacts no fee except the portion of our time that we give to it.

The Bible gives numerous illustrations of prayer demonstrating how it helps us make connections with God. It can be used at any time or occasion; not just when we feel we are inadequate, or in fear of death.

Do you remember what the Christian poet, Alfred Lord Tennyson wrote about prayer?

> More things are wrought by prayer
>   than this world dreams of.
> Wherefore, let thy voice rise
>   like a fountain for me night and day.
> For what are men better than sheep or goats —
>   that nourish a blind life within the brain;
> If, knowing God, they lift not hands of prayer
>   both for themselves and those who call them friend?
> For so the whole round earth is every way bound
>   by gold chains about the feet of God.

Let us use the Prayer Channel, *Channel One*.

102. Christmas Eve From Outer Space

The astronauts on *Apollo VIII* were exploring outer space around the moon, but they were men who also recognized God as Creator. It was on Christmas Eve 1968 when they made it possible for us, on Earth, to watch with wonder on television, as the cloud-covered Earth appeared from beyond the curvature of the moon.

At the precise moment astronaut Frank Boorman read from the Holy Bible, Genesis 1:1-10 (I summarize from the King James Version):

> In the beginning God created the heavens and the earth,
> And the earth was without form, and void; and darkness was upon the face of the deep. And the Spirit of God moved upon the face of the waters.
> And God said, "Let there be light," and there was light.
> And God called the light Day and the darkness he called Night. And the evening and the morning were the first day.
> And God said, "Let there be a firmament in the midst of the waters and let it divide the waters from the waters."
> And God called the firmament Heaven, and the evening and the morning were on the second day.
> And God said, "Let the waters under the Heaven be gathered together unto one place, and let the dry land appear," and it was so.
> And God called the dry land Earth and the gathering together of the waters God called the Seas, and God saw that it was good.

Surely all of us watching that spectacular moment felt closer to God than ever before. What a striking way to celebrate Christmas Eve in 1968!

103. Church Attendance

> Some go to church to take a walk,
> Some go to church to laugh and talk;
> Some go there to meet a friend,
> Some go there their time to spend;
> Some go there to doze and nod,
> The wise go there to worship God.
> — Anonymous

104. Church Attendance 2

We disagree with the news media on where most people attend events on Sunday. Consider the State of Ohio.

The total average attendance of just one denomination, the United Methodist Church, on a given Sunday, from both the East Ohio and West Ohio Conferences, would fill the Ohio State University stadium more than twice!

Add to that the attendance of Roman Catholics, Presbyterians, Baptists, Lutherans, Episcopalians, and the United Church of Christ, plus the twenty or more other groups, not forgetting the Charismatic Churches, and you can readily see four or five million people together.

Contrast that with the numbers gathered at arenas, such as the Cincinnati Reds, the Cleveland Indians, and the smaller stadiums found in Columbus, Dayton, Akron, and Toledo; they will not come near the church totals.

Questions: Which group, churches or sporting events, receives the most money? Which group influences the moral standards and core values of society the most?

Think about it.

105. Colorful Pottery And Adversity

God permits adversity, just like an earthly father may permit his child to fall and get hurt, in beginning to ride a bicycle or learning to skate.

Go with us to the pottery shop. Here we see various pots, plates, and vases with some dull paste markings. They are placed in a kiln, and after hours have passed they are removed, showing colorful blues, reds, or other hues of color.

How does the color get into the clay? The potter speaks with a twinkle in his eye: "The fire put it there."

Adversity can bring out better qualities of our soul, if we let God work through it. Jesus provided it for us.

106. Conscience

In the hallway of Eastern College, St. Davids, Pennsylvania, there hangs a most unusual college diploma. The name of the one who had once received it had been removed.

The student sent it back to the college several years after graduation time. In a letter he confessed that he had cheated on exams and did not deserve the diploma.

The school officials studied the matter, then returned it to the man, informing him that they were rewarding him for being so conscientious. But the individual still would not keep the diploma, and sent it back the second time.

Today it hangs there, name removed, to remind students of the value of a good conscience.

107. Contrasts In Character

Notice the sociological study of two families:

I. The Jonathan Edwards family:
He was a noted clergyman in New England in early America.
Of his descendants:
    13 college presidents
    65 college professors
    100 clergymen
    60 doctors
    100 lawyers
    30 public officials: senators, mayors of cities, and others

II. The Jukes Family:
He was a criminal of that same era.
His descendants included:
    300 who died prematurely
    200 thieves and murderers
    300 were executed for crimes committed

90 prostitutes
145 alcoholics
200 who were seriously diseased

This family cost New York State over $1,000,000 at the time the study was made, after World War II.

108. Cry, The Beloved Country

Alan Paton's book, *Cry, The Beloved Country*, suggests a valid answer to racism. Briefly, the black preacher's son in a province of South Africa had left the countryside to obtain work in the big city, only to fall into evil ways and to kill a white man. A striking fact of the matter was that the man he murdered was the son of the white landowner back in the same valley from which the black youth had come.

The redeeming factor came from the one who had lost his son.

Mr. Jarvis, the landowner, did not seek vengeance on the black people. Instead, he set out to make life better in that rural community. Employment would be offered so that the youth would not have to go to the big city. Better educational opportunities would be offered. Other changes were made.

The moral of the story: We who are privileged can offer opportunities to other persons, and thus help fulfill their dreams.

109. Education And The Ends

Education in life deals with ends:

Your head sits on one end, and you sit on the other.
Success depends on which end you use the most.
It's "heads up you win, tails you lose,"
So heads up! Get with it!

110. Eternity

So live that when thy summons comes to join
The innumerable caravan that moves
To that mysterious realm, where each shall take
His chamber in the silent halls of death,
Thou go not, like the quarry-slave at night,
Scourged to his dungeon, but, sustained and soothed
By an unfaltering trust, approach thy grave
Like one who wraps the drapery of his couch
About him, and lies down to pleasant dreams.
— William Cullen Bryant

111. Father's Day And The Trinity

The Trinity: three in one,
    John was a man's son.
    To himself he was a person,
    To his son he was a father.

112. Food For Thought

    There was a healthy controversy in England over a newspaper editorial that criticized a particular preacher's preaching. Then a parishioner wrote in complaining about the fact that he had faithfully attended worship services at his church for fifty years, and in all those years he could not remember a single sermon. He thought the preachers had done nothing to inspire him. For several weeks, letters appeared in the "Letters to the Editor" column, pro and con, about some preacher's sermons. Nothing seemed to quell the controversy.
    Then this letter came from a sincere person who preferred not to sign his name:

"Dear Editor:

I have been married to the same woman for the past fifty years. In all those years she has faithfully prepared my meals day after day. I cannot, in all honesty, remember any specific menu she has prepared. Sometimes, I cannot remember what we ate just yesterday. All I know is that day after day, year after year, she has given me nourishment, and I thank God for it."

After the letter appeared, there were no more letters sent in about preachers.

113. For A Dead Rabbit?

It was the season of the year when snow melts and springtime rains had raised the nearby stream to flood stage. Several people stood on the bank watching the angry swirl of fast-moving water. A boat was fastened to the tree at the bank.

One fellow spied a rabbit out on an island in the flood. He said, "I'm going out to that island in the boat and get that rabbit!"

"Don't try it; it is too dangerous," someone said.

But the man went to the boat, got in, untied it from its mooring, and began to row it, as strong as he could, to get to the island. It was not easy to do, but he made it. He retrieved the rabbit, put it in his hunting coat pocket, and again entered the boat to go to the shore.

But the rushing stream upset the boat, and the man was dragged under by the water and was swiftly carried away. They found his body about a half mile downstream, caught in some shore debris.

One of the men who found him pulled the dead rabbit out of the dead man's coat pocket and said, "That's what he gave his life for!"

What would we give our lives for?

114. For Thoughtful Worship

On the dossal cloth behind the central altar of the New Haven United Methodist Church in Indiana, are these words from Revelation 22:1: "A pure river of water of life, clear as crystal, proceeding out of the throne of God."
Simply remarkable! Worshipers appreciate it.

115. Forgiveness

To return evil for good is devil-like,
    To return evil for evil is animal-like,
To return good for good, is man-like,
    To return good for evil is God-like.

116. Four Things A Man Must Do

Four things a man must learn to do
    If he would make his record true:
— To think without confusion clearly;
— To love his fellow man sincerely;
— To act with honest motives purely;
— To trust in God and Heaven securely.
                  — Henry Van Dyke

117. Give Them Christ

In a letter from the publicity office of Tennessee Ernie Ford, shortly before he passed to eternal life, I read that Mr. Ford, a United Methodist, was lending his support to publicizing a new painting by a contemporary artist, Kenneth Wyatt. The painting was titled *Give Them Christ*.
The artist had chosen a scene at an ocean port. John Wesley was sending some of his methodist preachers to be missionaries in

America. Wesley, in his journal, reported that the incident had historical significance. When they asked him what they were to do in the venture, he had said to them, "Give them Christ."

What a fine thing for Tennessee Ernie Ford to do, help publicize this new work of art, and assist giving Christ to the persons interested in paintings. Mr. Ford had always ended his television program with a hymn when he was quite popular many years ago.

Can we do less than "Give Christ" to those whom we know?

118. God Bless America

A late nineteenth century Jewish immigrant, from western Siberia to the U.S., was the universally well-liked Irving Berlin. His composition, "God Bless America," had been written for a musical, but it didn't fit right, so he had laid it aside.

But when the rumble of war in Europe threatened to encompass the world, Mr. Berlin brought out the composition and had it published in 1938. Kate Smith was a popular music singer on radio at that time, and she helped to popularize "God Bless America."

It took off immediately, and became sort of an unofficial national anthem during the days of World War II.

Since that time it was less popular; until September 11, 2001, when terrorists forced our nation into another war. Probably no other musical composition has been used to express how Americans feel in the aftermath of 9/11. Easily memorized and sung, the chorus is:

God bless America, land that I love.
Stand beside her and guide her through the night with the light
    from above.
From the mountains, to the prairies, to the oceans white with
    foam,
God bless America, my home sweet home;
God bless America, my home sweet home.

Our fervent prayer would add *Amen*.

119. God Knows

David, the famous sculpture by Michelangelo, is now located in a museum in Florence, Italy. It is mounted on a pedestal, making it high and impressive. It is the crowning piece of the great artist's works. We were told how he worked painstakingly on every detail, even on parts of the figure that do not normally show, like the top of the head.

When he was asked why he did so, Michelangelo replied, "God knows!"

120. God Uses Written Prayers Also

In the late 1940s, Reverend Peter Marshall, the well-known pastor of the New York Avenue Presbyterian Church, Washington, D.C., was voted into the office of Chaplaincy of the United States Senate.

But the office required that the daily prayers, used while the Senate was in session, be prepared several or more days in advance of their use. This was requested by the office of the Reporters of Senate Debate, and the Congressional Record.

Peter had always prayed extemporaneously before, and was troubled about it. He and Catherine, his wife, visited a famous citizen of Washington, D.C., Mr. Starr Daily, and asked of him his idea of using written prayers. Dr. Daily assured Peter that God could tell him better what to pray in the quiet of his pastor's study, than in the hubbub of a noisy Senate chamber. The advice proved to be of great value.

God surely did assist Peter Marshall in writing in advance, and in praying those prayers at noon, the regular time. In fact, the prayers were so well-worded that it made Peter famous.

Men who used to vacate the chamber after the business session began staying for them. The media took it up and the nation heard about it.

At the time of convening of the 81st Congress, Peter prayed a 23 word prayer ending with the words: "God ... have mercy upon them."

Senator Arthur Vandenberg of Michigan said to Peter, "Now I know how a condemned man feels!"

But think of it, that prayer had been written several days before it was used!

121. Gratitude At Sing Sing

One of the classic stories of prison ministry pertains to the loving service given by Kathryn Lawes, wife of the famous Warden Lawes at Sing Sing Prison, New York, many years ago.

For seventeen years of her life, Mrs. Lawes was a daily visitor to the men incarcerated there. They let it be known to new prisoners that she was a true friend of all who came there.

She became close to those who needed extra attention, when there were problems in prisoners' families. She was a trusted confidant if one needed to share a special matter with somebody. She helped needy families back home.

When a tragic accident took her life, the convicts asked if they could view her body in the church *outside* prison walls. What a tremendous request that was!

But the Warden sensed their love and respect for Kathryn, and granted permission for them to go in single file, outside the prison, into the church where her body lay, a moment to pause there, then back in single file to the prison.

It was a marvelous fact that all who wanted to pay their respects to Kathryn Lawes were able to do so, and not a man broke that promise!

What a testimony to their gratitude shown that day in Ossining, New York.

122. Ground Zero — One Year Later

Listening to and watching television on September 11, 2002, as that long list of over 2,800 names was being read, of persons who lost their lives on "Nine/Eleven Day," we could sense some of the soul force people felt that day at that site in New York City. It was more than emotional.

And when the names of people from other countries were read as well, we were reminded that it had been a *World* Trade Center. The consequences of the tragedy affected representatives from nations around the globe. Enough were there to create an awesome spectacle. Now, the result seems to be deadly silence.

Parallel to that thought, as one visits the Dead Sea in the Holy Land, one sees and touches physically a body of water so loaded with chemicals one could hardly drown in it. No marine life can exist in such a place. Since it is far below normal sea level, and there is no outlet, one understands why it is named the Dead Sea.

But this unusual sea has something to give up to us. There is so much salt, sodium chloride, in the Dead Sea, the water can be piped out to flat ponds and allowed to evaporate in the hot sun. The result is then refined for various uses. Other chemicals are there also, just for the taking.

Centuries of water flowing down from Mount Hermon in Lebanon, through the Jordan River, have brought these precious resources to the Dead Sea.

Back to Ground Zero, one can see how much it is like the Dead Sea. Though once a site of lively trade offices, it has become a place of remembrance. These memories have developed a soul force that can have far-reaching consequences. After due respect is given to those who died through no fault of their own, it will surely give impetus to those who may develop that space in the midst of a great city.

Abraham Lincoln once said, "It is for us to be dedicated to the great task remaining before us, that from these honored dead we take increased devotion to that cause for which they gave the last full measure of devotion."

123. Growth

One little inch won't make you tall,
    You've got to keep on growing;
One little prayer won't do it all,
    You've got to keep on praying;
One word won't tell them what you are,
    You've got to keep on talking;
One step won't take you very far,
    You've got to keep on walking.

— Anonymous

124. He Drives Like Jehu

Someone has said that the modern American man's love for his automobile may yet be his downfall. If statistics prove anything, they report that one is safer traveling by a ship at sea or by a jet plane, than in the latest modern car, especially in an SUV (sports utility vehicle).

The expression in the Holy Bible we use to describe driving excessive speeds, "He drives like Jehu," comes from 2 Kings 9:20. King Jehu of Israel was driving his chariot "furiously." He has many followers today.

The manufacturing companies insist that they are doing all they can to make automobiles a safe means of transportation with better tires, visibility, and lighting. The modern highways are smoother than ever. It seems like something must be done to slow down the drivers.

An Ohio State Trooper told me that on holidays, he and another Trooper drove side by side on the Ohio State Turnpike at the proper speed, in order that they might slow down the traffic. In an accident where four teenagers died, the car had been traveling 93 miles per hour when it met an unmovable object, and the odometer was stuck at that point.

We have heard of State Troopers stopping drivers who were traveling over 100 miles per hour. Sometimes that occurs when drivers are under the influence of alcohol or other drugs, but it has been happening when there was no drug problem. If a car moving at 55 miles per hour is covering fifteen feet per second, how many more feet would it be moving at 100 miles per hour? There is no way accidents could be prevented at such a speed.

What can be done about it?

Along with the usual efforts for strict enforcement of the law and persons speeding excessively being dealt with more emphatically, I suggest that we follow the example of the effort to curb smoking. Society must insist that bad driving is *socially not acceptable*. Culturally, we have made smoking "not the thing to do" and we can also make dangerous driving "not the thing to do." Driving like Jehu can endanger other people's lives as well as that of the driver.

There are human lives at stake, and who knows, yours might be at stake as well as mine.

125. He Gave His Lunch

One of the great stories of the Holy Bible is the story of Jesus feeding the 5,000. I liked especially the part about who gave the loaves and the fish (John 6:9). Can you visualize it with me? It is the story of the lad who shared his lunch with Jesus.

Use your imagination with me of how the boy might have told his mother at the end of the day: "Hey, Mom! I saw it happen! I gave Jesus and his disciples my five barley loaves and the two fish. Jesus prayed about it, and then he began breaking the bread into pieces, and the fish were used, too! I'm glad I gave what I had; and all of us had something to eat!"

If all Christians would share what we have like that, the world would all have something to eat.

126. Highways To Happiness

A self respect that bears an honest name;
A mind content, a conscience free from blame:
    An inner poise, a will to teach the good;
A friendship shared, a duty understood.

    Contempt for fear, the dauntless heart of youth;
A hope of love that builds on faith and truth.
    These are the highways —
    Broad ways, the byways —
    These are skyways that lead to happiness.
— Anonymous

127. His Very Simple Credo

"To believe that there is nothing more beautiful, more profound, more sympathetic, more reasonable, more manly, and more perfect than Christ. Not only is there nothing, but I tell myself with jealous love, there can be nothing."
— Fedor Dostoevski

128. How A Child Thinks

A little boy went with his mother to see the movie *Snow White and the Seven Dwarfs*. They entered the dark room late, just in time to see the old witch give Snow White the poisoned apple.

They got through to the end of the movie, and stayed on to see the first part of the movie in its second showing. When they came to that scene again, with the old witch, the mother arose and started out of the theater, with the little boy in her hand.

But he kept looking back over his shoulder, and said to his mom: "If Snow White eats that poisoned apple again, she's crazy!"

129. How Did The Apostles Of Jesus Die?

Matthew — slain by the sword in a city of Ethiopia.
Philip — hanged at Hieropolis, Phrygia.
James, the Great — beheaded in Jerusalem by order of King Herod.
James, the Less — thrown from a pinnacle of the temple.
Bartholomew — whipped by imperial command and died of his wounds.
Andrew — starved to death, bound to a cross.
Thomas — slain with a lance in the East Indies.
Jude — shot by arrows.
Simon Zelotes — crucified in Persia.
Simon Peter — crucified, head down, in Rome.
Matthias — stoned and then beheaded.
John, the Beloved — died a natural death at Ephesus.

— Traditional

130. How Did You Play The Game?

When the last great Scorer comes
    To write against your name;
He writes not how you won or lost,
    But how you played the game.

— Grantland Rice (Sports Editor)

131. How To Handle Criticism

Gary Moore, an early television personality, used to tell how he handled a letter of false criticism. He said, "I sent it back to the writer with these words on it: 'Someone has been using your name in the mail, so I am sending the letter back to you so you can stop them from doing harm.' "

132. In The Presence Of God

It was reported that the great concert pianist Paderewski never went before an audience until he had spent half an hour in prayer, in communion with Almighty God.

Noted Premier of Poland in post-World War II days, as well as being a great musician, he knew the value of practicing the Presence of God.

After prayer he would go on stage and play the piano as few have ever played it.

133. Into Eternity

While touring Europe, you may visit the Cathedral in Milan, Italy. The building, built many years ago, was constructed with huge arches over the sanctuary.

Notice the words used (translated from Latin) on the arches:

Over the first arch are the words — "All that pleases us but for a moment."

Over another arch are the words — "All that troubles is but for a moment."

Over the central arch you will see the words, best of all — "That alone is important which is eternal."

134. Is The Bible A Bank?

Is the Bible a bank at your house? A wealthy woman, before her death, gave her Bible to a grandson and asked him to read it. He took it with him and cast it aside in his house with other miscellaneous items.

As life passed there were hard times, and he often had to do without things he needed.

Later in life, he picked it up, that old Bible, and decided to read it through.

Much to his surprise the man, now well along in years, discovered checks written and signed by his grandmother! Worthless, now, they could have been of much value to him in his younger days.

Is the Bible a locked-up book with much value (if we really read it)? Or is it just a strange place for money or other miscellaneous items?

135. Is This True Americanism?

Among the various things that have happened in the elapsed time since September 11, 2001, there has been too much false patriotism expressed against Muslin Americans. Over 860 incidents happened in the year after that tragic event that makes sincere Americans quite unhappy, and we are hopeful that such acts against these citizens will cease.

It was bad enough when some so-called Christians attacked American Jews because they had different religious views. Now the same tactics have been used against Muslim Americans. In its milder form, this includes such things as stones thrown at mosques and spray paint used to deface buildings dedicated to the worship of Allah.

From its beginnings, America has been a virtual melting pot of persons with diverse concepts of religion. One of our nation's strengths has come from standing together against evil forces in our society. The universal concept of conscience, of moral right and wrong, is not for one superior class or race in our land. All religious faith share a common sense vision of what "ought to be," and that has helped us develop fairness in America.

It must be made clear to the offenders that they can and should be brought to justice in our land where freedom is not a thing to be violated.

136. It's A Serendipity

Taken from the old Arabian fable, "The Princes of Serendip," we get the word "serendipity." Haven't you had an unexpected gift, an unusual pleasure, something not planned for of much value come to you in your life? Some may think of it as a windfall, if it is an economic surprise they have received.

Here are some examples of serendipity.

Hank Ketcham, a newspaper cartoonist, came home from work one day to find his wife in tears. She said, "Our son, Dennis, is a menace!" The result has been a very popular cartoon on the newspaper comics page.

Or there was the man who placed a piece of meat between two pieces of bread and found that it tasted very good. We use that man's name when we do what he did. He was the Earl of Sandwich.

Charles Goodyear had smeared a piece of raw rubber with sulphur and left it near a hot plate he had been using. Up to that time, though rubber had been used somewhat to waterproof clothing, it was too unstable to be considered practical. The next morning, Goodyear found that the piece of rubber was solid! The sulphur had solved his problem.

Jim Gamble of the Procter and Gamble Soap Company was hunting for a name for the new soap they had made. Though it floated, such slogans as, "It floats, 99% pure," did not catch on. Then one Sunday he was listening to the choir in his church sing "Ivory Palaces," and it rang a bell in his brain. The word "Ivory" ...! You know the rest of the story. That was a serendipity.

Spiritually, the grace of God given to all who believe in Christ is a serendipity. We cannot earn it or buy it; it comes because God loves us.

Look back on your life; thank God for the serendipities you have had.

137. Jesus' First Miracle

A converted alcoholic was asked if he believed the Bible story of how Jesus changed water into wine.

The alcoholic, now freed from addiction, said, "I don't about that, but I do know that when Jesus came into my heart, he changed beer and wine into food and furniture for my family; and that's a good enough miracle for me!" (See Gospel of John 2:1-11.)

138. Keokuk's Answer

At Keokuk, Iowa, we walked out on a high earthen dam, bolstered by concrete. This dam reaches across the Mississippi River, at a strategic place. The city has been a shipping port, both north and south.

While other cities up and down the mighty river have floods quite often, sometimes endangering residents and valuable properties, Keokuk is safe and dry.

Not only that, the dam includes a hydroelectric plant which generates power needed in the city. Power is also sold to other cities nearby, including southeastern parts of the state. Isn't it good to know that such energy can be placed under direct control in flood season?

Other cities on the river are not so fortunate. Residents of one city said a wall between the city and the river would tend to destroy the beauty of nature, and defeated the proposal. Humankind is not always wise in the way things are done or not done. So they fear the floods at springtime.

How do we control the powers of the human spirit? Might we find productive ways to use our human resources, and prevent destructive forces that come to us from time to time?

139. Kindness — Dale Carnagie

Dale Carnagie once said, "I shall pass this way but once: any good, therefore, that I can do, or any kindness that I can show to any human being, let me do it *now*. Let me not defer nor neglect it; for I shall not pass this way again."

140. Kindness — Emily Dickinson

Emily Dickinson wrote, "If I can stop one heart from breaking, I shall not live in vain: if I can ease one life the aching, or cool one pain. Or help one fainting robin into his nest again, I shall not live in vain."

141. Let's Roll! (No Greater Love Than This ...)

The last words of Todd Beamer of Cranbury, New Jersey, from United Airlines flight 93 to his wife may well take their place in time, along with "Remember Pearl Harbor," and "Remember the Alamo."

It was the morning of September 11, 2001, when hijackers had taken over this jet plane. The only contacts to the country below were being made by passengers to relatives by cell phones. Passengers called loved ones and spoke nervously, some more than once. The hijackers didn't stop them.

Aboard Flight 93 there were forty passengers including the crew, besides the three hijackers. At 9:45 a.m. Todd had talked by Airphone with a phone supervisor in Oak Brook, Illinois. He explained that three hijackers were in control of the plane: two had gone into the cockpit, while the other one was seen wearing a bomb fastened to his waist.

Tom Burnett, a passenger, had a conversation with his wife Deena, in San Ramon, California, reporting the knifing of a passenger. Later on, Deena told Tom about a plane hitting the World Trade Center.

He answered, "Oh, my God! It's a suicide mission!" Deena called 911 in the interim and reported to authorities, who did not know anything about Flight 93. Tom told Deena some of the passengers were going to do something.

There was no talk about ransom money. The plane had changed direction and was flying faster than normal and at a lower altitude. The news media, later, had enough information to believe that at least Todd Beamer and Tom Burnett, with other passengers, planned either to recover control of the plane or divert its directions. Todd's last words heard by the phone supervisor, Lisa Jefferson at Oak Brook, Illinois, were to someone on the plane: "Okay. Let's roll."

An Al Qaeda manual, obtained by the Associated Press after the tragic day, recommended hitting buildings with a high number of persons inside. It is now believed the intended target was the nation's Capitol building.

So the passengers, by their own concerted effort, were able to keep the jet plane from reaching Washington, D.C. It flew over U.S. Highway 30 southeast of Pittsburgh, Pennsylvania, and finally crashed outside Shanksville, in an open field.

What can we say about the heroism of those passengers who knew what their destiny would be? — Sure death!

We think of this Bible verse: "Greater love has no man than this, that a man lay down his life for his friends" (John 15:13 NRSV).

It certainly was proved that day in rural Pennsylvania.

142. Like A Candle

Continued worship of God can be like making a candle. You begin it with a good piece of string as the center. That alone would not give you a steady, lasting glow. We saw what can make a good lasting glow in a candlemaking plant.

If the cord is dipped repeatedly in tallow, it will build up into a nicely-shaped candle which will glow for hours.

It is the repeated dipping and bathing in the sources of energy that will make light possible.

So, with our souls before God in worship — time after time, time after time, time after time....

143. More On "Accountability"

Yehudi Menuhin, the famous concert violinist, was to perform in a New York concert hall. When the curtain opened, he seemed to be oblivious to it all: though intently listening to his accompanist. Suddenly he seemed to come alive and began to play the violin in a marvelous way.

Later, when asked what happened, he answered, "I suddenly realized that the violin I could not hear was my own!"

144. Most Unusual

The church is the only institution on earth that will let you in free, and then trust your honor to pay.

Movie theaters won't do it; ball parks certainly won't do it; and we never heard of a store that would let you help yourself and fill your basket, and then take a collection as you pass outside.

You wouldn't ride a train or a jet plane that way; they must be assured of their pay.

The church is entitled to such assurance also.

— Anonymous

145. Music, A God-given Grace

Have you ever thought what life would be like without music? We just take it for granted, much like some of the other graces God has given to humankind, such as prayer and our sense of conscience.

We listen to the great philharmonic orchestras, and are impressed by the excellent music that can touch us as nothing else can do.

God, in creation, gave us song birds which help us enjoy nature all about us. In fact, music is a universal expression not bound by human barriers of race, social class, nationality, or other things that can be divisive.

Much of the entertainment world uses music as a background for their theme: radio, television, and the theater thrive on it. No wonder that music has played such an important part in our lives.

The book of Psalms, in the Bible, has numerous references to both vocal and instrumental music. Psalm 150 gives a summary of such music in the days of King David, who was a harpist and is credited with having produced many of the psalms himself.

The church hymnal is a vital book we use for singing hymns, gospel songs, and choruses. This, along with scriptures and prayers, draws us closer to God.

We also read in the Bible about Jehosaphat who sent musicians before his army, expressing confidence in the power of God. It did have an effect on the enemy (2 Chronicles 22:21-22, 28-29). Today the military forces use music for various purposes, including entertainment, as a way of bringing unity in the services they represent.

Let us give God our grateful appreciation for music.

146. Of What Kingdom Are You?

A Sunday school teacher in the classroom asked the children this question: "Of what kingdom is a dog?"
Someone answered, "The animal kingdom."
Then the teacher asked, "Of what kingdom is a tomato?"
The answer came quickly, "The vegetable kingdom."
The teacher continued, "Of course; what kingdom is gold?"
The answer from several children was, "The mineral kingdom."
"To what kingdom do you belong?" asked the teacher.
Several wrong answers were given like, "The United States," or "Ohio." Then, with sudden inspiration one boy called, "Teacher, I know! I belong to the kingdom of God!"
Dear reader, of what kingdom are you?

147. Old Age — Browning

Robert Browning wrote:

Grow old along with me! The best is yet to be!
The last of life for which the first was made.
Our times are in His hand who saith, "A whole I planned,
Youth shows but half, trust God, see all, nor be afraid."

148. Old Age — Longfellow

Henry Wadsworth Longfellow wrote:

He has achieved greatness who has lived well,
    laughed often, and loved much:
Who has always looked for the best in others
    and given the best he had;
Whose life was an inspiration
Whose memory is a benediction.

149. On A New Year's Day

This passage was spoken by the King of England in World War II several times on the British radio broadcasting system to bolster the people on a war-weary day.

"I said to the man who stood at the gate of the new year, 'Give me a light that I may tread safely into the unknown.' "

And then he replied, "Go out into the darkness and put your hand into the hand of God. That shall be to thee better than light and safer than the known way."

150. On Saying Thanks

A boy's imagination knows few limits. It soars with wild freedom through the universe of space ships and rocketry, to dinosaurs and on and on. It may, however, run into a hard wall of common sense, as per this example:

A boy aflame with big ideas said to another: "What would you do if a space ship landed in front of you, and out stepped a man from Mars and handed you a million dollars?"
The other boy scratched his head, and said, after a moment of thought, "I'd say, 'Thanks.' "

As Christians in a prosperous and wealthy nation, we can learn from that story.

151. One American Dollar

While we were on a trip to Israel with a Christian tour group, we were amused by the peddlers of various items we might buy. They would call out: "All you need to buy this (item) is one American dollar!"
One of the tour group jokemakers coined a new so-called Bible verse: "One Lord, one faith, one baptism, and one American dollar!"

152. Our Total Trust In God

Dr. Ralph Sockman, for many years the pastor of Christ United Methodist Church, New York City, had a great description of how the Christian faith works. Said he: "If we take the parts of an ocean liner, one at a time, and put them in the ocean, they would sink to the bottom. Consider a huge motor, or a single piece of the hull: they would both sink. But when all parts are assembled in their proper place, and attached to each other as a working project, the ship will float."

We may not understand all that there is to know about the things of Almighty God. We ask, "Why?" about so many of them. Like "Why do the good people suffer?" or "Why do the wicked prosper while the hard-working, totally sincere people, often do not get their fair share in life?" "Why are there so many wars?"

God has things and beliefs yet to be seen and used. Some day we may see some of the answers, and maybe not. If we accept all in total trust in him, it will prove itself. Like when *all* the parts of the ship were assembled, it worked. (See Romans 8:28 NRSV.)

153. Parable Of The Ten-inch Skillet

Some men went on a fishing trip. An old bachelor went along and caught fish also. When he caught one, he would measure it with a pocket measuring tape, and throw any large fish back in the water. It made the others wonder.

Finally, someone asked, "Why do you keep only the smaller fish?"

He answered, "I have only a ten-inch skillet."

Moral of the story: Let us not forget witnessing to persons we might have thought were of lesser value in God's kingdom.

154. Pocketbook Protection

A pastor preached a sermon on that text in Ephesians 6:13-18 (NRSV), where there is a listing of the spiritual armor God provides for the believer. "Put on:

- the belt of truth around the waist,
- the breastplate of righteousness,
- and shoes on your feet, make ready to proclaim the gospel of peace,
- take the shield of faith,
- take the helmet of salvation,
- and the sword of the Spirit, which is the word of God."

But an astute Christian layman, a businessman, pointed out that the Devil could strike the man from the rear with flaming arrows and penetrate the hip pocket. That's where his billfold is! He may need pocketbook protection.

155. Poor/Rich Boy

The late Albert Schweitzer was a famous medical missionary to Africa, as well as a musician and theologian. Why would such a great man spend the prime years of his life ministering to poor black people in such a place when he could have achieved a name for himself in classical music or as a teacher in a theological school in Europe?

He told this story:

There once was a boy, the son of a well-to-do father. He wore nice clothes, lived in a nice house, and ate very good food. One day he got into a scuffle with another boy who lived down the street. The other boy came from a poor family, lived in a cheap house, wore ragged clothes, and had less to eat than had the first boy. The rich boy won the scuffle.

The poor boy dusted himself off and said that if he had food to eat like the rich boy had, he could have thrown down the rich boy. The rich boy never forgot the experience because he knew quite well that what the other boy had said was true.

From that day on he revolted against any favored treatment just because he was rich. He even dressed in cheaper clothes, and endured the hardships of the poor whenever it was likely he could.

That boy grew up to become the famous Dr. Albert Schweitzer.

Ezekiel 3:15 suggests that same spirit. Not a bad idea for us.

156. Practical Christianity

I simply argue that the cross be raised again at the center of the marketplace as well as on the steeple of the church. I am recovering the claim that Jesus was not crucified in a cathedral between two candles, but on a cross between two thieves: on the town garbage heap; at a crossroad so cosmopolitan that they had to write his title in Hebrew, and in Latin, and in Greek ... at the kind of place where cynics talk smut, and thieves curse, and soldiers gamble. And that is where churchmen ought to be, and what churches should be about.

— Reverend George MacLeod

157. Puppies Can Share, Too!

A doctor found a little dog with a broken leg by the roadside. He had compassion on him, took him home, put his leg in splints, and kept him until he was well. Then the dog began to run around the house. In a few days he disappeared.

"That's gratitude," thought the doctor. "As long as he needed me, he stayed, but when he didn't need me, he ran away."

But the next day there was a scratching at the door, and there was the little dog, and he had another dog with him, and that little dog was lame!

158. Redemption — A Drop Of Water

Do you remember in your childhood looking up and trying to understand the clouds? There were times when the sun's rays at the edge of a cloud would highlight a beam shining through the moisture between the cloud and earth. We kids would say, "The sun is sucking up water into the cloud." That idea gives us a hint of the meaning of redemption.

A drop of water lay in the mud, stained and polluted. But the sun shone down upon it, and drew it up into the skies, so that with many other little drops it could fall again to the earth, purified and truly a blessing.

God takes up to himself from our sick and worn-out bodies our souls to be cleansed by God's Spirit and then given a new life, eternal life. That is redemption also.

159. Ring Those Bells!

It was springtime in 1799, when Napoleon laid siege on the city of Feldkirk, Austria. On Easter Sunday, as was their custom, the bells in the church tower rang out that it was time for worship.

The Army of Napoleon heard those bells and concluded that the Austrian Army must have arrived in the city, and they turned away.

Easter Bells had saved the city!

160. Romans 8:28

"And we know that in all things, God works for the good of all those who love him, who have been called according to his purpose" (NIV).

If there was ever a time when this Bible verse had tremendous significance, it has been during the time that has passed since the tragedy of September 11, 2001, fell on America.

The God who brought the most positive force of redemption ever known, from the tragic death of his Son, Jesus Christ, on the cross of Calvary, is again at work in the lives of persons: yes, persons in all different denominations and religious faith organizations. We also consider persons with various racial heritages and different nationalities, as they tell us they feel his Divine Presence.

We are hearing more frequently how redemption is coming to persons whose lives were shattered by the loss of a loved one, either in the twin towers of the World Trade Center in New York City, or at the Pentagon in Washington, D.C., Many stories have appeared in the news media about what people have done in the elapsed time since "Nine Eleven." Surely God is at work in their lives.

Support groups have sprung up in places such as lower Manhattan, New York City, and in the nation's capital city. People come together to share their stories and to comfort each other. Slowly they are working their way out of their grief.

Many persons were bitter and cried out, "O God, why did you do this to me?" or "Why did God let this happen to me?" as they faced the reality that their husband or wife would not be coming back to them. Some of them, now, can see that God is at work in their lives for good. Some, now, can even smile again.

Some have had pastors or priests or rabbis help them to understand that though God permits tragic things to happen, he does not want things to be that way. When evil persons set out to commit premeditated murder, such as the events on "Nine Eleven" were to be, satanic forces were at work. In this world of moral freedom, evil choices were made with far-reaching consequences.

What else could it be but God at work in the lives of the volunteers who stepped up to assume tremendous responsibility, all the way from giving aid to exhausted firemen by preparing food and refreshment for them as they came off duty at Ground Zero to offering child care for a parent who had lost a loved one.

How grateful we all must be to know that God is for us and with us in any moment of our lives. That is true redemption, a gift of God's eternal love. Consider again. Romans 8:28, from the New International Version of the Bible.

161. Say It With Flowers

Henry Penn, the man who coined the phrase, "Say it with flowers," told Dr. William Stidger this true story:

Two boys and a girl came into Penn's Flower Shop and said: "We're a committee, and we'd like to get some nice yellow flowers."

The florist showed them some inexpensive ones. "Do they have to be yellow?" he asked.

"Yes, sir. Mickey would like 'em better if they was yellow. He had a yellow sweater," one of the boys said.

"Are they for a funeral?" asked Mr. Penn. The boys nodded and the girl made an effort to hold back her tears.

"She's Mickey's sister," a boy explained. "He was a good kid but a truck hit him. We saw it happen."

Said the other boy, "We kids took up a collection and got eighteen cents. Would roses cost that much? Yellow roses?"

The florist was touched and said, "I have some nice yellow roses and they're eighteen cents a dozen this morning. I'll make a nice spray with ferns and ribbon. Where shall I send them?"

"We'll take them," said the boy, "sort of give them to Mickey at the funeral home. He'd like it better that way."

The florist accepted the eighteen cents and the committee of two boys and a girl walked out to go to the funeral home.

Mr. Penn told Dr. Stidger, "I felt uplifted for days! I had the privilege of giving, and it left an afterglow on me."

Could we give an "eighteen-cent spray of yellow roses" to someone in our lives today?

162. Say, "Who Do You Love?"

The Youth Fellowship of the Epworth United Methodist Church of Lima, Ohio, used to have an interesting initiation ceremony using the words of our title above. One by one they would be ushered into the meeting room as into a solemn court. The President of the Fellowship would welcome them, and after a few pleasant remarks would ask the question: "Say, 'Who do you love?'"

Caught off guard there would be such answers as "My mom" or "My family"; or the youth might even name a boyfriend or girlfriend. The question was tricky and very few would ever say it right, by answering, "Who do you love?" They were not actually asked to give names. It was a lot of fun when they caught on to it all. The initiation was a good way to introduce the new person to the Fellowship.

We might ask ourselves that question, and then go on to get it right. That would lead us to consider persons we love.

(Proper grammar would be: WHOM do you love, but who uses it in conversation?)

163. Second Springs

In the 1930s, I lived in Sugar Grove, Fairfield County, Ohio. The Ohio Fuel Gas Company had two gas compressor stations: one was west of the town, the other was east, along Rush Creek and Logan Hill.

On a path along the side of the creek, north of the Logan Hill plant, there were two freshwater springs. On a hot, summer day, what a delight it was to pause and have a cool, refreshing drink at First Springs.

But when the hot, dry days of late summer arrived, sometimes First Springs would go dry. To get a drink of water, you would have to go on to "Second Springs" where artesian water flowed the year around: in winter or summer, spring or fall.

To me, in later years, I could see a lesson there for all of us. Spiritually, we need more than an initial gift, like that given by First Springs: too often showing in a nominal relationship, an erratic, or no attendance, at worship services at the church.

Name it what you will, we need to get to the place where there is a continuous witness of God's Spirit in our lives, like a drink of water from Second Springs which flows continuously. Too often we fail because we do not press on with faith in the living Spirit of God. Read what Saint John wrote in his Gospel, John 7:37-39 (NRSV).

"On the last day of the festival, the great day while Jesus was standing there, he cried out, 'Let everyone who is thirsty come to me, and let the one who believes in me, drink. As the Scripture has said, "Out of the believer's heart shall flow rivers of living water." ' [Isaiah 12:3]. He said this about the Spirit, which believers in him were to receive."

Yes, go on to the "Second Springs" and drink deeply of God's abiding love. Let it flow out of you in loving service to others who may need it desperately.

164. Seed Investments

Dr. Lloyd Bertholff was academic dean of Western Maryland College, when I first learned of his way of planting seed. I was attending theological seminary next door to that campus. He later became President of Illinois Wesleyan University, and continued his investments there also.

As a portion of his contribution to God each year, Dr. Bertholff would provide a fair scholarship for some worthy student who might not have been able to get an education otherwise.

For more than thirty years, he planted the seed of investment in young lives. Later, I heard him at a conference witness to what he had been doing through the years.

At first, he had little assurance that it was meeting the need for worthy students; but as the years passed, the seed began to grow, and proved to have been an outstanding way to make an investment.

As college education costs have accelerated, it has been of great benefit for some future leaders of the world. Our gratitude is hereby expressed to other persons who, like Dr. Bertholff, have also planted the seeds of investment, by scholarships for the youth of our land.

165. Selah

Question: In the book of Psalms in the Bible, what does the word *Selah* mean?

Bible teacher answered: "Let that soak in!"

166. Some Good Things Take Time

About the middle of the nineteenth century, a noted English traveler, Lord Sandys, was served a fine sauce in a restaurant in Bombay, India. He took the recipe back to England and asked Lea and Perrins, famous manufacturer of condiments, to duplicate it.

They did their best, but when Lord Sandys tasted it, it was inferior. After several tries, Lea and Perrins banished the sauce to a barrel in their cellar and forgot it.

Some months later, someone else found the sauce and tasted it. By then, the flavor was marvelous, and Worcestershire Sauce was born! As they said, "Time has worked a miracle!"

The hardest thing for most of us to do is to let time work a miracle. It happens time after time.

167. Stab Us Awake

Robert Louis Stevenson, a sufferer himself, wrote:

If I have faltered more or less
    In my great task of happiness;
If I have moved among my race
    and shown no glorious mourning face;
If beams from happy human eyes
    have moved me not; if morning skies,
Books, and my food, and summer rain:
    Knocked on my sullen heart in vain —
Lord, thy most pointed pleasure take,
    and stab my spirit broad awake!

168. Strangers?

A young married woman had been quarreling with her mother-in-law, to the extent that the elderly one had quit attending their church.

Yet, one afternoon, when children were in school, these two women were surprised at the movie theater to find themselves seated side by side, when the lights came on for the interlude when projector needs were being met.

They sat there as strangers and had a friendly conversation until the room darkened again. The younger woman told me about it in a counselling session.

But, would you believe that they took up their quarrel again after that experience?

God will have to settle situations like that!

169. Teamwork

Some years ago the Council of Bishops of the United Methodist Church met in Columbus, Ohio. At an evening dinner, special music was provided by the Otterbein College Choir, from Westerville, Ohio.

The Master of Ceremonies for that program was, at that time, the football coach of The Ohio State University, Woody Hayes, who was a United Methodist church member.

After a fine musical number by the choir, Woody said a very significant thing, as only a football coach might say it: "That was a perfect example of teamwork!"

170. Thanks For The Boll Weevil

At Enterprise, Alabama, there is a most unusual monument worthy of consideration. The inscription on the monument reads:

In profound appreciation of the BOLL WEEVIL
and what it has done as the herald of prosperity,
this monument was erected by the citizens of
Enterprise, Coffee County, Alabama.

Why? Because people in time of crisis found a better way.

The boll weevil had been so destructive to the cotton plant, it had threatened the income of people living on cotton plantations. Today the agricultural business in the southern United States is diversified, such as raising peanuts and potatoes as well as cotton.

Sometimes we must thank God for adversity. In Alabama, they thanked the boll weevil for forcing them to change.

171. That Sunday School Class Teacher

"Pastor," he had said, "I think I should be teaching that Sunday school class."

These were the words of a businessman, who a year earlier had been challenged to teach a class for young adults. He said then that he would have to study the Bible first.

We shared with him some Bible outlines, which covered the entire Bible in a book-by-book study we had been using with older adults. He promised to use them in preparation.

I had nearly forgotten about it when Bob Ash came to me in my pastor's study at the church. It was a real joy to hear him tell what that year of living with the Bible meant to him.

Mr. Ash had become the teacher of the Young Adult bible class at Trinity United Methodist Church in Delphos, Ohio. He taught effectively until his untimely death four years later.

But, oh, the joy of a year of studying the Bible with a definite purpose.

172. That Wedding Ring

The wedding party had proceeded down the center aisle of Epworth United Methodist Church, Lima, Ohio, led by a five-year-old boy as the ring bearer, and his six-year-old sister as flower girl. After finding their places at the chancel rail, the rest of the party included, the ceremony began.

Now, for a five-year-old boy, what the adults about him were saying and doing meant very little, so he began to release the ring from its pillow in the little box he was carrying.

Suddenly the ring popped up and fell down on the floor, where it began to roll toward a furnace cold air vent, some five feet away. The best man saw what was happening, wrenched himself away from us, and darted for the wedding ring, hoping he could catch it before it dropped into the cold air vent. He missed it, but at least deflected it from its course, and was scrounging around to capture it.

The wedding audience turned from watching us, who were almost to the ring ceremony, and began snickering, then laughing at the gyrations of the best man. The little boy began to cry, so his mother came forward and took him away to another room.

It took some time before we all quit laughing and could settle back to the solemn vows, "with this ring I marry you, in the name of the Father, and the Son, and the Holy Spirit."

From that wedding on, in our ministry, we made sure that the best man carried the wedding ring and the ring bearer had a mere substitute!

173. The Cleansing Fire

An impressive moment came, in the lives of many youth, on the night at church camp when they would gather, late in the evening, before the camp fire.

They had been instructed, during the evening meal, to write on a slip of paper, things in their lives they would like to be relieved of. We could call them sins.

There was some singing of gospel choruses they all knew, followed by the camp director giving a short, but meaningful, message on the cleansing power of the Holy Spirit. He likened it to the fire that was before them.

As the large pieces of wood became hot coals of fire, the youths were allowed to move forward and throw their list of undesirable things in their lives on the fire.

It was a soul-stirring moment for those who took it seriously. Their sins were gone, taken away by the cleansing fire of the Holy Spirit.

May it also be true for us today, to do the same thing, casting away all that hinders us from doing God's will (Hebrews 12:1).

174. The Dog Knew Best

A man who was an alcoholic had a dog which he loved very much.

But one day the dog jumped up in his lap, smelled his breath, turned around, and jumped down.

It struck the man very hard. Even his pet dog turned from him because he was an alcoholic!

He became a Christian as a result of that experience, and then he and his dog were the closest friends.

Must it take a pet dog to reveal to us our need?

175. The First Sunday School

Robert Raikes was no fatalist. He saw a need for the children of Cloucester, England, to study the Bible. He used every talent he had to encourage the children who came to him for the study on Sunday mornings.

They came, and the idea spread throughout the country.

Now, there are Sunday Schools in nearly all churches in all the nations of the world where it is permitted.

Actually, the public school system grew out of it, especially in America.

On Mr. Raikes' monument in London, England, are engraved these words:

"I said, 'Can anything be done?'
A voice said, 'Try.'
I did try and lo! What hath God wrought!"

The Bible no longer needs to be a closed book for children, because of what Mr. Raikes did.

176. The Fool Who Signed His Name

Years ago, Reverend Henry Ward Beecher said he received a letter of criticism, and the last page had on it only one word, "Fool."

Beecher's comment was: "It was the first time I have ever received a letter from anyone who signed his name but forgot the message!"

177. The Four Levels Of Life

1. The level of instinct.
2. The level of duty.
3. The level of receiving grace through faith.
4. The level of faith working through love.
    — Dr. E. Stanley Jones (*In Christ*, Abingdon Press)

178. The Good Neighbor

Have you ever had a time in your life when you were totally helpless? It may happen suddenly.

A woman, with a carload of children, felt her car skid off the road into a ditch six feet deep and full of water. She was able to get out of the car. "But how about the kids?" she thought.

Only with the help of a bread truck driver who saw her plight and stopped were they able to rescue all of the children before the car sank below the water's surface. The driver was a true neighbor in a time of need.

179. The Holy Bible And Pitcairn Island

Do you remember the movie *Mutiny on the Bounty*?

It was based on the true story of that island in the Pacific Ocean, and how it was changed by the reading of the Bible.

There had been six native men, ten women, and a fifteen-year-old girl on the island when nine soldiers were forced off the ship to live there. The *Bounty* went on its way without them.

One of the sailors discovered how to make beverage alcohol, and the whole colony suffered from drunkenness and sin.

One sailor, Alexander Smith, found a Bible. In fact he was the only sailor left, surrounded by native women and half-breed children. By studying the Bible, God's Word, he found Christ, and that made all the difference.

Twenty years later, when the outside world finally contacted Pitcairn Island, the colony was thriving, a community with no drunkenness or crime. There was no illiteracy, so all could read and write. The redeeming Grace of God, found through Bible study, changed everything.

180. The Inspired Holy Bible

1. It is not the concepts of just one man or group.

2. There are things given in the Scriptures that no human intelligence could have foreseen.

3. Its concept of Deity contrasts greatly from that of other gods; only divine inspiration could have given it to us.

4. The concept of Messiah and soul salvation is the theme of the Bible, written over approximately 1,400 years. There is nothing like it anywhere else.

5. The Bible would hardly dare to say it was divinely inspired if it were not so.

6. The uniform affection of all classes, races, cultures, and nations through the centuries is evidence it is from God. Psalm 23 has such uniform and universal appeal.

7. When all the world is segmented and prejudiced, and social forces on all levels are not with each other, it is good to have God's Word to bind us together at God's throne of grace.
— Summary from Dixon's *Analytical Study Bible*, 1966 edition

181. The International Garden Of Peace

In almost the exact center of North America, on the border of Canada and the United States, at the joining of the Province of Manitoba and the State of North Dakota, there is a beautiful place with 2,000 acres of trees and flowers. It is known as the International Garden of Peace.

Beneath the flags of Canada and the United States, there is a stone cairn on which are these words: "To God in his glory, we two nations dedicate this garden, and pledge ourselves that as long as man shall live we will not take up arms against one another."

The caregivers of the garden are members of the Order of Eastern Star.

If Canada and the United States can so live, the rest of the world can do so also.

182. The Love Of Christ

A Roman Catholic saint once said, the love of Christ is:

"as wide as the limits of the universe,
as long as the ages of eternity,
as deep as the abyss from which He has redeemed us,
and as high as the throne of God itself."

183. The Mayo Clinic

The world famous Mayo Clinic had a religious origin. In 1883, Dr. William W. Mayo was a practicing physician in Rochester, Minnesota, when what they called a "cyclone" hit the town. Today, we say a "tornado."

Dr. Mayo was given charge of an emergency hospital for people needing aid. The Sisters of the Order of Saint Francis worked with him. Later, it became St. Marys Hospital and Dr. William W. Mayo its superior officer.

From those beginnings has come the famous Mayo Clinic today, with facilities reaching out to three other states in the U.S.A.

The first officers were Dr. William J. Mayo and his brother Charles, sons of Dr. William W. Mayo. Since we believe all healing is divine, the Mayo Clinic is still a high level blessing to God and man.

The first blood bank in the United States was established there, and the clinic doctors were awarded the Nobel Peace Prize. The Clinic has cared for over four million patients, and will continue the same level of care in the future.

They were the first clinic to organize specialty services like thoracic surgery and dermatology.

It was brother William J. Mayo who said, "At this clinic the best interest of the patient is the only interest concerned."

There is no doubt good reason for Mayo Clinic to be considered the top medical and surgical care center in the world.

184. The Miracle Of Ice

A Mrs. Lah, a missionary in a desert area of inner China years ago, reported a miracle as a result of prayer. Their doctor told a patient and friend that they needed ice to scatter an infection and lower the patient's temperature. Where in a desert would they get ice?

They prayed like Elijah (1 Kings 18:41-46), facing a hot August sun. The missionaries, the doctor, and the patient's wife, as well as the patient knew it would take a miracle.

Then the sky clouded up and rain fell on the parched land. The miracle happened as ice came in the form of hail, in copious quantity. The people gathered enough hail to meet the need. The infection was scattered, and the sick person was on the way to full recovery.

We have a God of miracles!

185. The Miracle Worker

Did you ever see the motion picture *The Miracle Worker*? A new version of it has been released. In the version years ago, Patty Duke played the part of the child Helen Keller, the world's most noted deaf mute.

All through the story, Miss Sullivan, the teacher, tried to communicate with Helen, who up to then had become a very stubborn and spoiled child. It was not until the dramatic scene of the two at the old-fashioned iron pump that any contact was made.

Miss Sullivan was pumping water in the hands of Helen, and then writing the word in the child's palm.

Suddenly, Helen began to say that word she had used when she was a baby, before her illness: WA WA, meaning water. It became what theologians call an "existential moment": a moment of reality, a great breakthrough.

It can be such a moment of reality for one seeking to know God, when one realizes that God is seeking us! He offers us forgiveness of our sins, a new life in Jesus Christ. The miracle of saving grace sets us free.

186. The People Had A Mind To Work

When the fires were finally extinguished, near Washington, D.C., at the Pentagon Building, which had taken such a severe blow on September 11, 2001, immediately the proper authorities set about to remove the damage and replace what had been destroyed.

The original building had been well constructed. In fact, some renovation was being done, particularly in that sector that had been hit. Architects and draftsmen worked overtime with new and stronger plans, which would bring life out of destruction.

Persons visiting the site observed how everyone went about their tasks with much fervor. They would rebuild, yes! And it would be a demonstration to the world what can happen when a true democracy is doing its very best.

There is a biblical parallel to all of this: In the book of Nehemiah, we have the story of Nehemiah, the cup bearer of King Artaxerxes of Persia. The king granted favor to Nehemiah to go back as the governor of Jerusalem, his home, and rebuild the walls of the city.

There is a fascinating story, of how opposing enemies — Sanballot, Geshem, and Tobiah — sought to stop the massive undertaking of the Jewish people. The task was completed in 52 days.

Back to the rebuilding of the Pentagon. By September 11, 2002, one year later, the huge project was completed, even to rebuilding the outside wall. Sandstone was used from the same quarry in Indiana where the original stone had been carved. It matched exactly the rest of the building! Once again the largest building in the U.S.A. represented the purpose the rebuilders had in mind, to confront the forces of satan with ultimate victory.

Like the builders of Jerusalem in 432 B.C., the people at the Pentagon *had a mind to work.*

187. The Prince Of Peace

Arthur Brisbane, a famous newspaper editor in the days of World War I, wrote philosophically on world peace:

"We may sweep the world of militarism. We may scrub the world of autocracy. We may carpet it with democracy, and drape it with the flag of republicanism.

"We may hang on the wall the thrilling picture of freedom: Here the signing of America's independence, there the thrilling portrait of Joan of Arc; yonder the Magna Carta, and on this side the inspiring picture of Garabaldi.

"We may spend energy and effort to make the world a Paradise itself: where the lion of capitalism can lie down with the proletarian lamb.

"BUT, if we turn into that splendid room mankind with the same heart, deceitful and desperately wicked, we may expect to clean house, just not many days hence. What we need is a peace conference with the Prince of Peace!"

188. The Prince Of Peace 2

At the close of World War I, there was a meeting of world leaders to discuss the future. President Woodrow Wilson from the United States of America was there and offered the plan for a "League of Nations," to work together for lasting peace. He was enthusiastic about it.

The French Prime Minister, Clemenceau, sneered at Wilson: "You talk like Jesus Christ!"

Yes, the League of Nations was a great dream then, and it faltered; but time has proved that President Wilson was right. He once said, "I would rather be defeated in a cause which one day will succeed, then be victorious in a cause which one day will be defeated."

189. The Print Of The Nails

The blind hymn writer, Fannie Crosby, gave an answer to a critic on how a blind person could believe in Christ when she could not see him.

Her answer was given in the chorus of a hymn she wrote:

I shall see Him, I shall see Him,
And redeemed by His side I shall stand;
I shall know Him, I shall know Him,
By the print of the nails in His hand.

190. The Seed Store

A man once dreamed he had entered a different kind of store. This one had in it gifts from God to humankind. There was an angel in charge.

The man went up to the counter and asked the angel: "Since I have run out of fruits of the Spirit, can you restock me?"

The angel responded, "We do not stock fruits; we only stock seeds!"

191. The Story Of Ben Hur

Two friends met at the Union Train Terminal in Indianapolis, Indiana, years ago. They were businessman Robert Ingersoll and retired army general Lew Wallace. Ingersoll was surprised to learn that Wallace took Christianity seriously, since to him it was mere superstition. But he so challenged his retired friend about his faith that Wallace actually traveled to the Holy Land.

There he walked where Jesus walked and he lived again the scenes in the life of Christ. Upon his return home, he wrote *Ben Hur*. It is a famous story based on the life of Christ, lived out in a person's life. The story was a best seller many years ago, and has been produced in film and video.

This is a testimony of Lew Wallace: "As a result of my research, I became convinced that Jesus Christ was not only a Savior of not only the world but that he was my Savior, too, and being convinced I wrote *Ben Hur*."

It is a story worth your reading or viewing in the third millennium.

192. The Vale Of Paradise

Mrs. Yocom and I have had the privilege of visiting some missionaries in Peru and Chile in South America.

One of the cities we visited was Valparaiso, Chile, and it is a beautiful city whose name literally means "Vale of Paradise." The harbor on the Pacific Ocean is beautiful and treacherous.

When storms come in from the southern seas, the ships have to move out into the open sea and face reality. What had appeared to us as a safe place could be a place of destruction, as the ship could be wrecked on unseen rocks.

Life is sometimes like that. Rather than be destroyed by the storms of human living, we must face reality, and be led to safety by God's Holy Spirit.

192. There's A Man On The Cross

When the Chicago Temple United Methodist Church was built, they placed on top of it one of the highest crosses above street level in the world.

But recently, there were a lot of excited people looking up from the street. Why? They actually saw a man on that cross.

It was soon made known to them that it was a roof repairman. The cross had been there day after day. People became interested *only when there was a man on that cross*!

What does that say to you and me?

194. They Cooked The Books

The new expression of what has been happening in some of the top business corporations of America well describes the effort to remove all incriminating evidence.

When the news media first told of Enron Corporation and its false front of prosperity, we could hardly believe such terrible things could happen. Not only was the business unprofitable, but all retired employees no longer had a retirement fund that they had trusted for their future income.

Then we learned that another huge corporation, World Com, was also in dire financial straits. And other businesses were in deep trouble. This did shake the business world so much that the stock market dropped to unheard of lows, and we wondered what could happen next.

That's when the expression, *"They cooked the books,"* was heard so frequently in the news.

If we look in the Holy Bible, we read that Moses gave this advice to the Hebrew children in their desert trip toward the Promised Land: "Be sure your sins will find you out" (Numbers 32:23 NRSV). The Old Testament prophets Isaiah and Ezekiel also echoed the concept in their prophecies.

Saint Luke, in his Gospel, quoted Jesus, "That which you have whispered behind closed doors will be proclaimed upon the housetops" (Luke 12:3 NRSV).

How terrible that innocent people are left destitute while those who "cooked the books" live on in the height of luxury.

Slowly, but surely, justice will prevail, even in the business world.

195. Those Two Cents

It was during the 1950s and the young couple came to their pastor for premarital counseling. When the groom-to-be inquired about the pastor's fee, the pastor said he would make them a deal. In those days the usual amount was $10.

"If you give me a check for $9.98 after the marriage ceremony, I will accept it. Three months later, if you think it was worth the money you gave me, I will accept the other two cents."

The pastor had forgotten about it, but on a Sunday morning three months later, after the morning service at the church, the groom handed the pastor two cents and they smiled.

Years later, they met again and agreed it had been a good deal!

196. Three Philosophies Of Life In The Story Of The Good Samaritan

1. What's yours is mine; I'll take it! — the thief
2. What's yours is mine; I'll keep it! — the priest and the Levite
3. What's mine is ours; I'll share it! — the Good Samaritan

197. True Brotherhood

A young black man was carrying two suitcases on a wintry day in New York City. His name was Booker T. Washington, who later wrote a classic of American literature: *Up From Slavery*.

A white man came alongside and helped Booker by carrying one of the suitcases to Grand Central Railway Station.

"That," said Booker, "was my first encounter with Theodore Roosevelt!"

No wonder "Teddy" was so well loved.

198. True Brotherhood 2

It is interesting to know that the New Testament of the Bible has taught the equality of all humankind, ever since the letters of Saint Paul were written. As Christians, we believe in the Bible being the inspired Word of God. Consider these verses from the New Revised Standard Version of the Bible!

Galatians 3:28 — There is no longer Jew or Greek, there is no longer slave or free, there is no longer male or female, for all of you are one in Christ Jesus.

Colossians 3:11 — There is no longer Greek or Jew, circumcised and uncircumcised, barbarian, and Scythian, slave and free, but Christ is all in all.

1 Corinthians 12:13 — For in the one Spirit we were all baptized into one body, Jew or Greek, slave or free.

Romans 10:12 — For there is no distinction between Jew and Greek, the same Lord is Lord of all.

And Saint John wrote, and we read, **John 10:16** — "I have other sheep that do not belong to this fold. I must bring them also, and they will listen to my voice." These are the words of Jesus, speaking to a gathering of Jews.

In the light of modern medical science we know that blood types are the same worldwide. Color is only skin deep. Curly hair and thick lips are external factors.

Education can bring up to equal the use of mental capacity, when opportunity is given to neglected races or nationalities. There is no such thing as a superior race. When we begin to live as equals, then there can be true brotherhood.

199. True Friendship

"Oh, the comfort, the inexpressible comfort, of feeling safe with a person: having neither to weigh thoughts nor to measure words, but pour them all right out just as they are, chaff and grain together; knowing that a faithful hand will take and sift them, keep what is worth having, and with a breach of kindness blow the rest away."

— John Oliver Hobbs

200. Twentieth-Century Evaluation

"They were very decent people, their only monument being a concrete road and 1,000 lost golf balls."

— T. S. Elliott

201. Wahlstrom's Wonder

Some yeas ago, a man by the name of Wahlstrom made a machine that got news media attention. The machine was quite a contraption to behold!

It had bells, lights, motors, pulleys, wheels, and gears. It looked and sounded impressive, and was called Wahlstrom's Wonder: the bells rang, the lights flashed, the motors ran, and the gears and wheels moved, but the machine did not amount to anything. There was no end product!

What does this new millennial age offer? We hear a lot about the computer and the internet. People get addicted to these new gadgets just like people of a past generation were addicted to television in its early days.

Will humankind ever learn that helpful as these electronic marvels can be, they will not necessarily bring in the Kingdom of God? But that will take an act of the soul and mind, and may we seek for it.

202. Was It Luck Or Pluck?

Some years ago, a famous Canadian ice skater, Barbara Ann Scott, won the highest honor a skater can have: she was a winner at the Olympics.

Someone was talking with her mother about how lucky Barbara had been to win. She asked, "How much did she practice?" The mother answered, "Barbara has spent 20,000 hours on her skates practicing during the last ten years!"

Branch Richey, a noted major league baseball team owner, who started Jackie Robinson on his way to breaking the race barrier in sports, once said, "Don't think a ball player is just lucky to have been the person who caused his team to win a decisive victory. That player may have worked very hard at learning the skills he used that day. He may have suffered defeat, he may not have always had good days when he played, but his persistence brought him to that moment of victory."

Life is like that. Not so much "luck" as "pluck."

If we wait to be lucky, it will probably not happen. Sheer luck drives many gamblers into debt. Only those in life with "pluck" will win at the end.

Do you remember the nursery story of the Little Red Hen?

203. What A Dream!

Camp Wesley, located six miles north of Bellefontaine, Ohio, was originally the site of a government environmental project. After a dam was built and a lake of more than twenty acres was formed, the Lima District of the Methodist Church bought it in the 1940s for church camping.

The sloping west shore of the lake was bare except for a few thorn bushes and some unsightly weeds.

Reverend Dwight Woodworth, a Methodist pastor from Tipp City, Ohio, had a dream of that bare land covered with evergreen trees. He convinced enough other people of the dream so that work did begin on that bare land.

A "Work Day" was scheduled when Boy Scouts from Tipp City, along with other volunteers, set out several thousand small evergreens on that hillside. The weather was favorable and now those trees reflect in the water by the light of a late afternoon sun.

Now we realize that pastor Woodworth's dream has come true to the glory of God.

May we, too, have such lofty goals for life.

204. What If The Christian Faith Was Gone?

There is a vital principle presented to us in a book by Henry Rogers; years ago he wrote *The Eclipse Of Faith*. There he set forth the idea that the influence of the Christian faith had been mysteriously wiped out. Nothing was left that touched people with Christ.

What about the many churches and Sunday schools? They were gone! Also, the para-church organizations, like the Salvation Army, and the YMCA, no longer existed.

He turned to art and discovered that all of the greatest paintings, such as Raphael's *Sistine Madonna*, and da Vinci's *The Last Supper* were gone; and all the best works of sculpture also had disappeared, for they were Christian in purpose.

The Bible was gone, as were the millions of Christian books; and devotional literature of all kinds were conspicuously absent from libraries, and even from people's homes!

So, too, with the finest of music: Handel's "Messiah" and the Bach "Chorales" as well as hymns and gospel songs were gone.

It touched every area of life. If we take away the Christian faith, we soon realize that the most effective forms of human understanding could not have reached their highest and best without the divine influence of Christianity.

What if the *Eclipse Of Faith* presented by Henry Rogers came true? There are forces in our world who have threatened to cause it to happen. Can we believe that enough persons will not let that happen?

205. What One Man Can Do

The Roman Catholic monk, Polemicus, dared to oppose gladiatorial death in the Coliseum of Rome.

Though the Emperor, Constantine, had ruled such acts of carnage were wrong, after his death, when a century had passed, Christians were being destroyed by gladiators in the Coliseum, with even emperors present for the scenes.

But one day, after a bloody exercise before a huge crowd, it stirred this Roman Catholic monk so greatly that he left his place in the rows of seats and was next seen out in the arena. He began to shout to the crowd and denounce what they had witnessed that day.

One version of the story says that Polemicus challenged others to join him before the gladiators. Slowly others came and joined him, until there were more of them than there were gladiators on the field.

The Emperor was there that day and was deeply stirred by the courage of Polemicus. A royal decree was sent out banishing the murderous gladiatorial scenes, and never again was there such terrible carnage in the Coliseum.

Martin Luther in his great hymn, "A Mighty Fortress Is Our God," expressed the God-given support Polemicus had received to be able to do what he did.

> The Prince of Darkness grim, we tremble not for him;
>   His rage we can endure, for lo, his doom is sure
>   One little word shall fell him.
> Dost ask who that may be? Christ Jesus, it is He
> Lord Sabaoth His name, from age to age the same,
>   And He must win the battle.

206. What's Missing?

The newspaper reported that a new post office was built in a certain town, and the day was set for its dedication. After due ceremony that day, a person who had been designated came forward to deposit the first letter.

But something was missing! What was it? There was no mail slot through which mail could be deposited!

What's missing in our lives?

207. When Henry Ford Gave A Dime

Years ago Martha Berry, founder of the Berry Schools in the mountains of Georgia, visited Henry Ford. She asked him for ten cents! When he asked her why such a small amount was requested, Martha said, "I just want to show you what I can do with ten cents, Mr. Ford."

He gave her the dime and she bought some seed peanuts with it. These she planted and later harvested. The next season she replanted again the seeds from the first planting.

Mrs. Berry repeated the process for *four* years, and sold that crop for $10,000. Then she went back to see Henry Ford, the auto millionaire, and reported on the project. He was quite surprised.

"I just wanted you to know," she said, "what I can do with an investment. I have given everything I had to these Georgia mountain children, and I want you to do something for them also."

So Mr. Ford wrote out a check and gave it to her. It was for two million dollars!

208. Where Is God?

Dr. E. Stanley Jones used to tell of a five-year-old child who was asked, "Where is God?"

The child put his hand over his heart and said, "In my heart!"

209. Where Is Your Goal?

In the Arabian Nights collection of stories, there is this one:

A young man dreamed of a place where there were "acres of diamonds." He was so impressed that he set out to find those diamonds. Years later, he returned to the home community, a broken man.

But now he realized that the man who bought his farm, by industrious hard work, had succeeded in reaping plentiful harvests each year from the soil, and that there were acres of "diamonds" right there!

Russell H. Conwell, a famous lecturer, was so inspired by this story that he prepared a great lecture on it, traveled the world, and gave that lecture over 6,000 times! It gave him "acres of diamonds" as well.

210. W(h)ite Out

Every author knows the value of this modern substance which can be used when we have typed the wrong letter or word, and need to make a correction. And as the years pass, we seem to need more of the W(h)ite Out, because we make more errors!

When an author gets caught up in his subject, words flow sometimes too fast, and we want to get it all down in black and white.

When using a pencil on paper we can erase the errors, but it is not that easy with a typewriter or a word processor. And even after our manuscript is finished, we know how important it is to have another person edit our work. The white fluid covers our mistakes.

We sin and make our mistakes, but Almighty God covers it all by the shed blood of Christ on Calvary. "Though your sins are like scarlet, they shall be white as snow" (Isaiah 1:18 NRSV). As the Haitian proverb puts it, "God's pencil has no eraser."

Thank God for Jesus and his Grace — and thank God for W(h)ite Out.

211. Who Is The Architect?

The day after a fire had destroyed a wing of the British House of Commons, many letters poured into Parliament, asking that it be restored exactly like it was before.

No plans were on hand for this restoration, so the call was sent out to find the architect who had built it.

An old man collecting paper in his attic for a scrap drive ran across some old blueprints he had made years ago. He was the architect and these were the plans of that wing of the House of Commons! He was able to solve the problem for his country.

Who is the architect for the plans of our world today?

212. Who Made God?

Children often ask profound questions over which we all stumble. A writer in the April 5, 1999, issue of *Christianity Today* magazine quoted a child's question while looking for a pretty flower. "God, if you are God, then you made everything. But, God, who made you? And who made that God?"

Some things we take on faith. As human beings we are unable to comprehend fully the concept of God. Only as we *experience* what God has done, and is still doing in the lives of people, can we begin to understand what God meant when Moses encountered him on Mount Sinai. God said, "I AM who I AM." To be I AM forever is surely beyond humankind's highest concepts.

In the Hebrew language, the verbal structure of "I am," is in a causative conjugation, meaning TO CAUSE. "I am" is not just as a being, which would be a *noun*, but as a *verb*, which would put God into action. He *causes* what is to be.

Saint John, who believed in the preexistent Son of God, wrote in his Gospel the I AM designation for Jesus, saying, "I am the Bread of Life; I am the Light of the World; I am the Door; I am the Way, the Truth, and the Life; I am the Good Shepherd! I am the Resurrection and the Life; I am the Vine."

When I think of how great God is, I like to remember that Jesus was God for us.

J. B. Phillips wrote a New Testament translation of the Bible worth reading; also since then, he wrote a book titled *Your God Is Too Small*. It will knock down some of our concepts that make God like human beings — like those who say God looks like Santa Claus, or the old man with a long white robe sitting on a throne away up in heaven.

Instead of wanting God to be like us, we should strive to be like God.

Like a child, we must go on through life learning more about the great God we have. We can tell children to look for signs of things God has done and is still doing. Creation goes on. Every time a baby is born, it is a new creation and we marvel how God has permitted it to be. And when a seed is planted and a new plant grows, it is another evidence of God in creation. We can say to a child that God lasts forever. God was God before us, and will be God after we exist. We read in Hebrews 13:8: "He came to us in Jesus Christ who was the same yesterday, today, and forever."

213. Who Really Pays The Tax?

One excuse for the sale of alcoholic beverages is that those who produce the drinks pay taxes. It is not so! The *consumer* pays. He may also pay sales tax on it. The beer and liquor producers pass on the taxes they may have to the price they charge for the product.

Just think of the positive benefits that could result if the money spent for alcoholic beverages was used to purchase food, clothing, and the necessities of life. Some people cannot afford both.

It also costs more for society to have police and the sheriff's department to protect the public from the deleterious effects of use of beverage alcohol. It is the consumer who pays, always.

214. Wisdom

On President Calvin Coolidge's desk these words were displayed:

"A wise old owl sat on an oak,
The more he saw the less he spoke;
The less he spoke the more he heard.
Why aren't we like that wise old bird?"

215. With God At Antarctica

When the famous explorer Shackleton reported on his explorations in Antarctica he said, "When I look back, I have no doubt that Providence guided us!"

His companion added, "I had a curious feeling on the march that there was another person with us."

Years later General Richard E. Byrd, from the United States of America, felt that same way in an experiment he performed in Antarctica, living in an isolated hut away from the rest of the explorers.

Read Daniel 3:24-25.

216. W.W.J.D.

Have you seen the initials W.W.J.D. on various objects, like bracelets and buckles, used by modern Christian youth? They stand for What Would Jesus Do? When faced with a moral decision of right or wrong, they find help in these words. They go on to think: Would Jesus get drunk? or: Would Jesus gamble? W.W.J.D.

Actually, it all goes back to the book *In His Steps* by Reverend Henry Sheldon, written many years ago. The idea is based on Scripture: "Because Christ also suffered for you, leaving you an example, so that you should follow in his steps" (1 Peter 2:21 KJV). In the book, Pastor Sheldon used the thought, "What would Jesus do in daily life, in business, and social affairs?"

Dr. Glenn Clark of Macalister College, after World War II, wrote a sequel *What Would Jesus Do?* bringing it into more recent times.

This concept of W.W.J.D. has also been helpful to many people in this new millennium.

Section III
Hope Windows For Life

217. Finally, There Is Hope

The phrase, "Hope springs eternal in the human breast," says a lot. Without hope we would be in a sad state of existence.

It is interesting to realize that hope is a universal blessing. Every culture on earth has a hope, if not for the best in this life, surely a hope for eternity.

Saint Paul listed hope as one of the three elements of a healthy spirit (1 Corinthians 13:13). Faith, hope, and love: the greatest of these may be love, but don't forget hope.

As the years pass we think more about the blessed hope, referred to in Saint Paul's letter to Titus, "having been justified by his [Christ's] grace, we might become heirs, having the hope of eternal life" (Titus, v. 37 NIV).

The Bible describes Heaven in various ways, earthly treasures lose their hold on us, and we long for something that is of lasting value. I quote from Revelation 21:3: "God himself will be with them, he will wipe away tears from their eyes, death will be no more; mourning and crying and pain will be no more, for the first things have passed away" (NIV).

Saint Paul quoted from Isaiah 64:4, when he wrote: "No eye has seen, no ear has heard; no mind has conceived what God has prepared for those who love him" (1 Corinthians 2:9 NIV).

Also, one of our joys for Eternity is our hope to know each other in a better time and place. I quote, "Then I will know fully even as I am fully known" (1 Corinthians 13:12 NRSV).

Great as it will be to be in Eternity, greater still it is to be assured that our many friendships will be continued there. I look forward to that wholeheartedly. And especially to be with our best Friend, the Lord Jesus Christ.

Do you remember that old gospel song, "The Eastern Gate"? There is a phrase that runs through it quite often: "I will meet you in the morning, just inside the Eastern Gate over there."

Psalm 30:5: "Joy comes in the morning."

So may it be.

218. The Eastern Gate

I will meet you in the morning,
    Just inside the Eastern Gate;
Then be ready faithful pilgrim,
    Lest with you it be too late.

If you hasten off to glory,
    Linger near the Eastern Gate.
I am coming in the morning,
    So you'll not have long to wait.

Keep your lamp all trimmed and burning,
    For the Bridegroom watch and wait;
He'll be with us at the meeting,
    Just inside the Eastern Gate.

O, the joy of that grand morning,
    With the saints who for us wait;
What a blessed happy morning,
    Just inside the Eastern Gate.

Chorus:
    I will meet you in the morning,
    I will meet you in the morning,
    Just inside the Eastern Gate over there;
    I will meet you in the morning,
    I will meet you in the morning,
    I will meet you in the morning over there.

— L. G. Martin

Section IV
Conventional Wisdom Windows For Life

A — Humorous One-liners

A1. Prejudice is being down on what you're not up on.

A2. You get ulcers not from what you are eating, but from what's eating you.

A3. All that I am or will be, I owe ...

A4. Advice to speakers: KISS — Keep It Simple, Stupid!

A5. Time wounds all "heels."

A6. You never know by the looks of a frog how far he can jump.

A7. Are you fun to live with?

A8. Would you make a better door than you would a window?

A9. Elbow grease gives the best polish.

A10. A harpist is a plucky musician who works his (her) fingers to the tone.

A11. If you just fiddle around, you'll never lead the orchestra.

A12. Patience is throttling your motor when you would like to strip the gears.

A13. A gossip: one who gives you all the details without knowing the facts.

A14. It's easy to see that you do not believe in "girth" control.

A15. Drinking and driving are putting the quart before the hearse.

A16. There's too much month at the end of the money.

A17. We ought to go to church to get a faith lift.

A18. Diplomacy is the art of letting someone else have your own way.

A19. In God we trust, all others must pay cash. (Sign in an old-time store)

A20. A miser is a fellow who never goes buy buy.

A21. If you want to get ahead, use your own.

A22. Sign in school classroom: "Time will pass. Will you?"

A23. When all is said and done, there is usually more said than done.

A24. Social Security: an old age insurance which guarantees you steak after your teeth are gone.

A25. Statistics show that the best time to buy anything was last year.

A26. A diet is a small matter, when you get mind over platter.

A27. The minutes you spend at the dinner table won't make you fat; it's the seconds that do it.

A28. Painting the pump does not change the purity of the water.

A29. A rut is a grave with the ends knocked out.

A30. If you are unhappy at home, you should try to find out if your wife hasn't married a grouch.

A31. Fishermen don't die; they just smell that way!

A32. Speeding is a habit ... brake it!

A33. Don't knock your church; it may have improved after you last visited it.

A34. Just keep smiling; people may wonder what you've been up to.

A35. How will you spend eternity: smoking or nonsmoking?

A36. Plan ahead: it wasn't raining when Noah built his ark.

A37. You won't find a funeral hearse pulling a U-haul trailer.

A38. A dog is loved by old and young; he wags his tail and not his tongue.

A39. What happens if you get scared half to death two times?

A40. Puppy love can lead to a dog's life.

A41. The nurse was criticized for being absent without gauze.

A42. An American is one who fills his garage with junk and leaves an automobile worth $25,000 sitting outside in all kinds of bad weather.

A43. Jesus said, "Blessed are the meek," not "Blessed are the stupid"!

A44. The best things in life are not always fat free.

A45. Stop your sniveling! (College bumper sticker)

A46. You are old when it takes longer to rest than it does to get started.

A47. Gossip is letting the chat out of the bag.

A48. There is a margarine for those who are past forty years of age called "middle-age spread."

A49. Life is one fool thing after another; love is two fool things after each other.

A50. People don't smoke; the tobacco does. People are the suckers!

A51. One of the best things in life to have up your sleeve is a funny bone.

A52. It has been reported that after death one of the so-called self-made men had said, "You know I never thought Heaven would be so hot!"

A53. A church layman said, "We pay preachers to be good; we laymen have to be good for nothing!"

A54. An expert is a "drip" under pressure.

A55. What do spooks eat for breakfast? Ghost toasties.

A56. If it ain't broke, don't fix it!

A57. Seen in a college girls' dorm in the 1940s: We are broom mates; we sweep together!

A58. Laughter is a fine tonic; don't bottle it up!

A59. Use your head; it's the little things that count!

A60. Sign on a child's stroller: "Please be patient; God isn't through making me yet!"

A61. Sign on a plumber's van: "We repair what your husband fixed."

A62. Car towing company sign: "We don't charge you an arm or a leg. We want your tows."

A63. Sign in front of a funeral parlor: "Drive carefully. We can wait."

A64. Seen in a beauty shop: "I'm a beautician, not a magician."

A65. Sign on a church bulletin board: "KWITCHERBELLYAKIN!"

A66. Sign in front of a church: "K-Mart is not the only saving place."

A67. Drive safely: Better late here, than up there!

A68. Drive thoughtfully: You may need seat belts only once!

A69. Drive carefully; and avoid the mourning after.

A70. Drive with care; you don't bet on the other guy.

A71. Definition of a baby-boomer adult: "He's stopped growing on the ends but not in the middle."

A72. Definition of a babysitter: "He's a teenager acting like an adult, so some adults can be out acting like teenagers."

A73. "Happiness is being married to your best friend." Steve Ragsdale, on Christian radio

A74. One farmer claimed it was so dry his cows gave powdered milk.

A75. He said it was so hot, corn popped in the fields.

A76. Another farmer said his chickens were laying hard-boiled eggs unless they were fed a ration of cracked ice.

A77. He said he had to tie knots in the pigs' tails so they couldn't slip through the barnyard fence.

B — Great Windows One-liners

B1. The best computer you'll ever know is the one between your ears.

B2. More doors are opened with please than with keys.

B3. Money buys a fine dog, but only kindness will make him wag his tail.

B4. A Bible that's falling apart usually belongs to a person who isn't.

B5. Life begins at forty, they say; but you will miss a lot if you wait that long.

B6. You can always accept a smile at face value.

B7. The shortest distance between two persons is a smile.

B8. Laugh and the world laughs with you; weep and you weep alone.

B9. He who laughs last laughs best.

B10. You will never find time for anything, but if you want time you will have to make it.

B11. Is your life a mission, or an intermission?

B12. The future is the time when you wish you had done what you are not doing now.

B13. On mystery: if we talked about what we understand, there might be a great silence.

B14. God has no grandchildren.

B15. Life's greatest tragedy: to lose God out of our lives and not miss him.

B16. Real freedom isn't free.

B17. The best things in life are not things.

B18. Some people read the Bible like a drunk who comes to a light pole — not for light, but for support.

B19. Religion isn't big enough; being good enough isn't either. Only Christ.

B20. Hope defined: that which is revealed by a dog when he wags his tail.

B21. You can do more than pray after you have prayed; but you cannot do more than pray until you have prayed.

B22. The Christian life is not a force pump but an artesian well.

B23. To try to forget is to remember.

B24. God invented love, but God won't mind if we borrow the idea.

B25. Any man can be a father, but it takes someone special to be a daddy.

B26. Keep the rumor going, God loves you!

B27. Starve a mosquito; give to the blood bank.

B28. Old adage: Seeing is believing, but we would add that sometimes "believing is seeing."

B29. There are no "answering machines" on the prayer line to Heaven; and the line is never "busy."

B30. A lot can be accomplished if we aren't concerned about who is going to get the credit for it all.

B31. Two hates never made one love affair.

B32. We have learned to fly airplanes like the birds, and to swim in the sea in a submarine like a fish; but it remains for man to walk this earth as men — brothers! (on a billboard in New York City).

B33. It is the overflow of the heart that gives the lips full speech.

B34. Consider the fish; he never gets caught so long as he keeps his mouth shut.

B35. It is marvelous what God can do with a broken life if you give God the broken pieces.

B36. The wishbone will never replace the backbone.

B37. Cars are not the only thing recalled by their Maker.

B38. FAITH is **F**orsaking **A**ll, **I T**rust **H**im.

B39. The majority isn't always right.

B40. In the church, it ain't the heat; it's the humility.

B41. Some live by the hourglass; others by the heartbeat. Take your choice.

B42. A smile takes but a moment, but its effect may last forever.

B43. If you help a Senior Citizen, you help one person; but if you help a child, you help a multiplication table.

B44. Two together shortens the road. — Irish Proverb

B45. The eye of a friend is a good looking glass. — Irish Proverb

B46. May the hinges of our friendship never grow rusty. — Irish Proverb

B47. May you live as long as you want, and never want as long as you live. — Irish Proverb

B48. If you drink, don't drive; better yet, don't drink! (The life you save may be your own.)

B49. Drive carefully; Heaven can wait.

B50. Snowflakes may be fragile, but see what they can do when they stick together.

B51. Sages of the ages agree, life is caring and sharing.

B52. Gratitude is the lubricant on the gears of everyday living.

B53. A train standing still costs money. (Maybe a church, too.)

B54. After all, the shortest road is the straightest.

B55. Success comes in cans; failures come in can'ts.

B56. Your journey with God begins with the first step, but don't let it end there.

B57. Sins may not be like scarlet; they may be just plain yellow.

B58. You can't turn the clock back; but you can wind it up again.

B59. Have no fear of growing old; many do not have the privilege.

B60. A Christian is a person who, when he/she gets to the end of the rope, ties a knot in it and stays there.

B61. If we haven't that within us which is above us, we will soon yield to that which is around us.

B62. If you're going to toot a horn, blow a trumpet for God.

B63. Give God what's right, not what's left.

B64. Before you go to bed, give your troubles to God; God will be up all night anyway.

B65. About dating: a gentleman is a guy who makes it easy for a gal to be a lady; and a lady is a gal who makes it easy for a guy to be a gentleman.

B66. He who has not Christmas in his heart will not find it under a tree. — Christmas One-liner

B67. Is Christmas a holiday or a Holy Day? — Christmas One-liner

B68. Wise men still seek him. — Christmas One-liner

B69. Jesus: the Reason for the season. — Christmas One-liner

B70. Whose birthday is it anyway? — Christmas One-liner

B71. Christmas star: God has a light in his window. — Christmas One-liner

B72. Please! No booze at Christmas. — Christmas One-liner

B73. Christmas, make the season bright. — Christmas One-liner

B74. Feliz Navidad. — Christmas One-liner

B75. We have just heard of a cemetery that raised its burial costs and blamed them on the higher costs of living.

B76. If you think your child's education is expensive, try ignorance.

B77. How we pity Satan, he can never love anybody!

B78. Did you know the 2003 calendar was so popular because it had so many dates?

B79. Today it's raining like cats and dogs; there are poodles all over the place.

B80. God is not limping on crutches. — Finnish Proverb

B81. God is not dead; somebody lied!

B82. The Eleventh Commandment: it's DO NOT HASSLE!

B83. The aim of life's game is to exalt his Name: the Lord Jesus Christ.

B84. Child in a Vacation Bible School asked, "Does God talk Spanish, too?"

B85. The turtle goes places when he sticks out his neck.

B86. My body was a tavern; now it's a temple. — Converted alcoholic

B87. May the Good Lord take a liking to you, but not too soon. — Irish Proverb

B88. If your God is dead, try mine! — Car bumper sticker

B89. All that glitters is not gold. — Anonymous (not in the Bible)

B90. Someone has said, "I am seriously interested in the world's possibilities, not its actualities."

B91. He who spits against the wind, spits in his own face. — Old American Proverb

B92. She has done what she couldn't. — Gravestone epitaph

B93. Many so-called open minds should be closed for repairs. (*Farmer's Almanac*)

B94. Grandmas are antique little girls.

C — One-liners From Notable People

C1. "He is no fool who gives that which he cannot keep, to gain that which he cannot lose." Jim Elliot, martyred South American missionary

C2. "So live that when you die even the undertaker will be sorry." Mark Twain

C3. "The modern church is too much like a football game; the players are seated in the bleachers, and the coach is alone on the field." J. T. Seamands

C4. "You can fool most of the people some of the time, but you can't fool Mom!" Spanky of *Our Gang* comedy

C5. "Keep a song in your heart." Lawrence Welk

C6. "O Lord, thou hast given so much to me, give me one thing more — a grateful heart." George Herbert, poet

C7. "The poorest man I know is the man who has nothing but money." John D. Rockefeller, Sr.

C8. "Think young, aging is for wine." Phyllis Diller

C9. "We might as well try Christianity, everything else has failed." George Bernard Shaw

C10. "God always finishes his sentences." Albert Payson Terhune

C11. "The test of courage comes when we are in the minority; the test of tolerance comes when we are in the majority." Dr. Ralph Sockman

C12. "Genius is ten percent inspiration and ninety percent perspiration." Thomas Edison

C13. "It is easier to restrain a fanatic than to revive a corpse." Bishop Arthur Moore

C14. "Never go to a doctor whose office plants have died." Erma Bombeck

C15. "Love is medicine for the sickness of the world." Dr. Karl Menninger

C16. "They had a weather office in Washington all these years and haven't changed the weather yet." Will Rogers

C17. "People who need people are the luckiest people in the world." Bob Merrill, songwriter

C18. "Tell me your certainties; I have doubts enough of my own." Goethe

C19. "It doesn't take much of a man to be a Christian: it takes all there is of him." Aldus Huxley

C20. "The Devil made me do it!" Comedian Flip Wilson

C21. "Happiness consists not in getting what you want, but wanting what you've got." Clara D. Wiggins, in *The Cabbage Patch*

C22. "Only those fit to live are those who are willing to die." General Douglas MacArthur

C23. "Cleanliness is next to godliness." John Wesley (not in the Bible)

C24. "God helps those who help themselves." Benjamin Franklin (not in the Bible)

C25. "Small things done with love can change the world." Mother Teresa

C26. "Ours is a world of nuclear giants and ethical infants." General Omar Bradley, World War II

C27. Definition of a Christian: "Giving and forgiving." Henry Van Dyke

C28. "I never met a man I didn't like." Will Rogers

C29. "God always leaves an unfinished task on the workbench of the world." William Allen White, newspaper editor

C30. "America may be humanity's last chance; certainly it is God's latest experiment." Peter Marshall, U.S. Senate Chaplain in the 1950s

C31. "God don't make no junk!" Ethel Watters

C32. "In Christ, life is no longer a **?**. In Christ, life is an **!**." Rev. George Campbell

C33. "If you tell the truth, you don't have to remember anything." Mark Twain

C34. "Aim at Heaven and you'll get earth thrown in; aim at earth and you'll get neither." C. S. Lewis

C35. "We have met the enemy and he is us." Pogo, cartoon character

C36. "Laughter is the shortest distance between two people." Victor Borge

C37. "The world has never been the same since God died!" Edna St. Vincent Millay

C38. "Love is contagious; we get it from each other." Ziggy, cartoon character

C39. "Plan to make the world a better place than it was when you came into it." Minta Yocom (my mother)

C40. "Evangelism is just one beggar telling another beggar where to find bread." D. T. Niles

C41. "The church is the only society in the world, the membership of which is based upon the single qualification, that the candidate shall be unworthy of membership." Dr. C. C. Morrison

C42. "God is not a 'Cosmic Bellhop' to run your errand." Dr. E. Stanley Jones

C43. "In Christ, I see the incredible, I know the unknowable, and I do the impossible." Dr. E. Stanley Jones

C44. "The right thing to do is the healthiest." Dr. E. Stanley Jones

C45. "Experience can be more meaningful than belief." Dr. E. Stanley Jones

C46. "The bud is prophecy of the flower." Dr. E. Stanley Jones

C47. "Love is never off duty; there are no moral holidays in being a Christian." Dr. E. Stanley Jones

C48. "In Jesus everything is opportunity, opportunity to make everything into something new." Dr. E. Stanley Jones

C49. "If you see a need, and you know you can meet that need, that is your call to Christian service." Bishop Richard Raines

C50. "Let go and let God." Paul Rader, evangelist

C51. "The buck stops here." President Harry Truman, in the Oval Office

C52. "Lord, please make me the kind of person my dog thinks I am." Rev. W. J. Keating, Arizona

C53. "There is always room at the top." Daniel Webster

C54. "The world is a kind of spiritual kindergarten where millions of people, bewildered infants, are trying to spell GOD with the wrong blocks." Edward Arlington Robinson

C55. "Let my heart be broken with the things that break the heart of God." Bob Pierce, founder of World Vision

C56. "Is that your final answer?" Regis Philbin

C57. "Man is the only animal that blushes or needs to." Mark Twain

C58. "It's never too late to be what you might have been." George Eliot

C59. "So help me, God." George Washington

C60. "Give me a hundred men; yes, give me ten men totally consecrated to God, and I'll show you what God can do." John Wesley